GUERR

MARKETING
FOR
FRANCHISEES

125 Proven Strategies, Tactics and Techniques
to Increase Profits For:

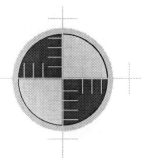

- ☑ Franchisees
- ☑ Licensees
- ☑ Authorized Dealers
- ☑ Real Estate Agents
- ☑ Manufacturers Reps and
- ☑ Mortgage Brokers

Jay Conrad Levinson
and
Todd Woods

NEW YORK

GUERRILLA MARKETING FOR FRANCHISEES

ISBN: 978-1-60037-025-0 (Paperback)
ISBN: 978-1-60037-065-6 (e-Book)
ISBN: 978-1-60037-133-2 (Audio)

Published by:

MORGAN · JAMES
THE ENTREPRENEURIAL PUBLISHER ™

Morgan James Publishing, LLC
1225 Franklin Ave Ste 325
Garden City, NY 11530-1693
Toll Free 800-485-4943
www.MorganJamesPublishing.com

Cover and Interior Design by:
Tony Laidig
www.thecoverexpert.com
tony@thecoverexpert.com

TABLE OF CONTENTS

FOREWORD

DO YOU KNOW how deliriously wonderful your life in the future is going to be like? I do. It's all described in the pages of this astonishing book. To be sure, it's not all peaches and cream, but then again, most of it will be.

To begin, let's agree that succeeding as a franchisee is not that easy, not that obvious, not that common. If it was, there would be no need for Todd and I to have authored this book for you. We know, by real life experience, that there are mistakes that many people make. You won't make any of them after you finish absorbing the wisdom in these pages. We also know that there are secrets that can propel you higher and faster than you may have dreamed possible. Those secrets are also presented to you here.

We've got to let you know out front that this book will do only half the work for you. Having the right knowledge is only half the battle. The other half resides in your ability to take action. Guerrilla Marketing is not a spectator sport. It's all about action—and that means you. We'll tell you what actions to take. We've even included a galaxy of worksheets to begin the momentum for you. Truth is, we've taken all the steps possible to make your success as certain and glowing as we can.

The right mindset? It's in these pages. The strategy that will lead you to your pot of gold? Also in these pages. The creativity to send your profits soaring? You're holding a book of it right now.

Todd has run a multi-million dollar franchise. I have consulted others on how to catapult themselves to the multi-million dollar level. The information is all there for you. It's failsafe. It's foolproof. It's surefire. But the most important part of our equation is you. Alone, you wouldn't be able to do it without these insights. Alone, these insights couldn't do it without you. It's the combination of the right information and the right action that's going to lead you to your promised land.

This is a book not only of truths about franchising, but of new truths, proven truths, practical truths. It may toss a glass of ice water into some myths you've been believing. But it will also spark a flame of passion and understanding.

Nowhere in this book do we say that it's easy. But we do say that it is possible. And we do say that you can do it. All that's needed is exactly the right information—presented clearly.

And that's what you've got in front of you right now.

We'd wish you good luck in your endeavors, but we know that luck has nothing to do with it. It's that elusive blend of smarts and action that's going to give you the gold. We're rooting for you on every page. And we're confident that you'll enjoy franchising and the money it earns for you. We've pulled out all the stops on your road to success. There's nothing stopping you now.

So let's get going!

Jay Conrad Levinson
The Father of Guerrilla Marketing

INTRODUCTION

I WAS RETURNING from a seminar in LA a few weeks ago. As soon as the plane took off most people put their seats back, grabbed a pillow or blanket, and tried to catch an hour of "shuteye". I was tired but I couldn't sleep. Instead, my thoughts were on franchise owners, you who have had the courage to go into business for yourself.

Going into business for yourself is quite a bit like stepping to the end of the "plank," so to speak, and jumping into the deep, dark, abyss of the unknown. This first step is a phenomenal accomplishment. Congratulations!

For me, when I bought my first franchise, it came very close to being my last step as well. I suddenly and unexpectedly found myself in a "gasping for air phase," trying to stay afloat. Fortunately, I became aware of Jay Conrad Levinson and his Guerrilla Marketing Tactics that helped change my mindset about the role of the franchisor and my role as the franchisee. In this book I share my learning experience with you.

Why Do Franchisees Need to Know More about Marketing? ...Doesn't the Franchisor Do it All?

In our years of research and recently on our radio program Franchise Boot Camp Radio, www.FranchiseBootCampRadio.com, where we interview the best of the best franchisors, franchisees, and franchise industry experts, we hear time and time again a widespread myth that goes something like this: "To be successful as a franchisee you just need to cut a check and work the business because 'corporate' will do the rest."

After interviewing all the big names from Burger King to Subway, Blockbuster Video, Jenny Craig, Chevy's, Villa Enterprises, and many others, all the findings indicate that those franchisees who truly succeed at taking their business to the highest level possible, are those who don't rely solely on their franchisor for success.

The franchisor provides the brand, the blueprint so to speak, and the basic tools for success, but at the end of the day, those franchisees who are the most successful don't expect too much from their franchisor. Instead, they embrace what they provide and build on it.

Most franchisors have a proven model for success. Use it. Follow it. Embrace it! But remember, you need to be the C.E.O. of your own business. Act as if everything depends on you. Take the marketing knowledge and ideas you learn in this book and fit them into what you are currently doing. You don't need to totally re-invent the wheel. Whatever you are doing to market your business, check it against the proven information in this book. We highly endorse and recommend that you get approval wherever necessary from your franchisor, if it is required, on new marketing ideas. Your relationship with your franchisor is extremely valuable.

You will notice worksheets throughout the book. Complete each exercise as you read along. Also, use the online resources at The Franchise Training Center www.FranchiseTrainingCenter.com. With the purchase of this book you received a password that will allow you 30 days unlimited access to the tools in the online center. Please use them. You will find details on your one-month free unlimited access on page 257.

Section One

GUERRILLA PREPARATION

THE WINNER'S CIRCLE

TEN YEARS AGO, I set out to buy my first franchise business. My partner and I signed up to be Jamba Juice area developers and signed an area development agreement for five locations in Phoenix, Arizona. I was pumped, completely jazzed about owning a multiple-location franchise business.

Over the next few months, we pulled it all together. I moved my wife and five kids 850 miles away from where we had made our home and opened the first Jamba Juice store in Phoenix, Arizona.

We shelled out over $400,000.00 for our first two locations opening them within only a few months of each other. According to our financial model and projections, the stores would pay for themselves within three to four years and we would have a cash flow coming in. I felt like I could finally live the American dream.

Then we held our grand opening. The doors opened and... nothing happened. No customers. Well, okay a few. But where were the lines with the people out the door? How was it possible that in 110 degree weather, the lines were not going around the block? They did at the other Jamba Juice stores I saw. In fact, the stores that spurred my interest in Jamba Juice in the first place were in less heat-intensive climates with customers waiting in long lines in the cold rain no less. Surely Jamba Juice was the ideal franchise with the perfect product for the wilting heat of Arizona. Where were the long lines of customers?

Here is where it gets ugly. I will never forget the day I had to make the call, the one to my financial partner telling him that we needed to infuse more money. It was gut-wrenching. We could not make the payroll. I had employees to pay and no money to pay them with. I could not understand it. I had vendors calling me for money. My food distributor refused to send me product unless it was C.O.D.

Then, it got worse. We had to keep shoveling money in to stay afloat. One year later we were forced to close our first location and relocate it. Three months after that we had to close our second. Our landlords charged us thousands of dollars to break the leases. I was frustrated. I was depressed. I was embarrassed. There we were 18 months into it and $500,000.00 in the hole with a huge cash flow problem.

One day, I had completely had it. I was at rope's end. I left work early to seek help from a book. Surely with all the marketing books out there I could find some help! As I was looking through the bookshelves at the bookstore I came across one of the first editions of Guerrilla Marketing. What in the world is Guerrilla Marketing? Who is Jay Conrad Levinson? I sat down and started to read.

To be truthful, this is the one book that helped me save my business. It was what I read in that book, the first edition of Guerrilla Marketing, and the principles I applied that helped me turn the corner at Jamba Juice.

My story actually turned out to be a success story. Our roots, hard work, and marketing finally took hold and we built the brand in Phoenix. Year after year the company's average growth was 6% per year in the 450 stores covering 22 of the United States. For three years straight, our five stores doubled that of the average.

Yes, doubled! With 12% growth on average, including during the tough year that followed September 11th.

It was a tough road but my partner and I turned the loss of half a million dollars into a thriving package of stores. We grew dramatically over the years that followed and then sold for several million dollars. How? By applying the principles we are covering in this book.

The story doesn't end there. I now have the privilege of working personally with Jay Conrad Levinson. In this book we combine our individual experiences to bring you the best possible information for Franchise Marketing Success.

PROFIT DRAIN

THIS BOOK has two objectives:

1. To teach you how to retain the customers you currently attract by plugging profit drains.

2. To teach you how to attract more customers in the most effective way using Guerrilla Marketing tactics.

Before we explore in detail more than 100 guerrilla marketing tactics, let's talk about these two objectives in more depth.

Here's the fundamental idea:

Marketing + Retention = Profits

Using the analogy of a bathtub to drive this principle home, let the bathtub represent your retained customers and profits. The tap and faucet on the tub represents the inflow of marketing to your business. How many marketing tactics are you using now? Are you relying on corporate, your franchisor, to do it all for you? Perhaps you are doing some direct mail, or magazine advertising.

If the approach I just mentioned is your approach, I'd venture a pretty sure bet your new customer inflow looks something like the following illustration with business SLOWLY trickling in. This approach will take a very long time to fill the tub.

The only problem with the slow approach is that franchisees also have the challenge of the drain, the "profit drain" that is. Sometimes

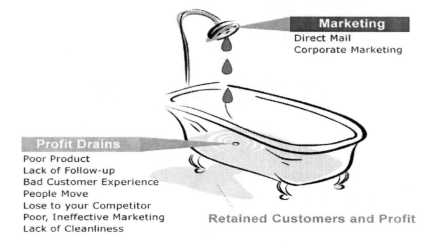

Marketing + Retention = Profits

Marketing
Direct Mail
Corporate Marketing

Profit Drains
Poor Product
Lack of Follow-up
Bad Customer Experience
People Move
Lose to your Competitor
Poor, Ineffective Marketing
Lack of Cleanliness

Retained Customers and Profit

we lose customers quicker than we get new ones. Reading the lower left corner of the illustration you'll notice:

Profit Drains can include:

- a poor product or service

- lack of follow-up

- a bad customer service experience

- people moving out of the area

- customers switching to your competition

- poor and ineffective marketing

- lack of cleanliness of a retail location

These are all reasons you may lose customers. How big is your profit drain? How many customers are you losing? Are you funneling more into your business than you are losing?

This is the challenge. Not only do you need to focus on increasing the amount of new customers coming into your business, you need to focus just as much on retaining them and keeping them happy.

How many of those profit drains can you control in your business? Take a look at scenario #2:

Marketing + Retention = Profits

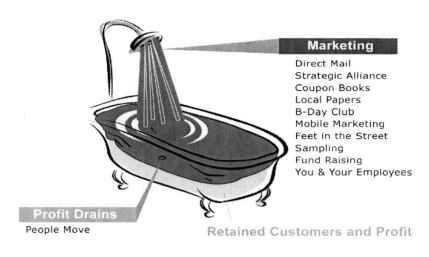

Marketing
Direct Mail
Strategic Alliance
Coupon Books
Local Papers
B-Day Club
Mobile Marketing
Feet in the Street
Sampling
Fund Raising
You & Your Employees

Profit Drains
People Move

Retained Customers and Profit

First, notice the tap. Wow! What a difference! In this scenario, rather than relying on one or two marketing tactics, many and varied strategies are employed. It has been proven time and time again, the more strategies you use the more new customers you will have coming through your business. Notice also, many of these marketing tactics don't require a lot of money. That is true Guerrilla Marketing.

Another important thing to notice is the drain itself. In this scenario the drain is mostly plugged up. Only one profit drain factor remains. The rest have been eliminated because they can all be addressed and corrected. You can control the quality of your product or service, your customer service, etc. The only thing you can't control is that people will move away from your trade area. Or is that really insurmountable? Actually a true guerrilla marketer would be mailing postcards to all the new move-ins in the area to replace those who move, but we'll get to that a little later.

As you learn more about the guerrilla marketing weapons and tactics available to you, keep in mind that a combination of at least 10 weapons and tactics must be used at all times to keep that tap flowing strong and steady!

Success Concept 3

SURVIVE OR THRIVE

The Essence of Survival

TO THRIVE, not just survive in today's business world, there is no room at the top for mediocrity. I really believe the saying, "Successful people do that which unsuccessful will not do." Clearly many franchise business owners are not willing to practice this philosophy. According to the American Association of Franchise Dealers, 15% of new franchise companies go out of business each year. That equates to 75% of new franchise businesses going under during a 5-year period. Of two million businesses that open their doors in the United States each year, 75% of them fail within the first five years. Why? There are many reasons, but let's focus on franchise businesses.

First, most franchisees discover they didn't really know how hard it would be. As a matter of fact, there are many who venture into the world of franchising who haven't thought through whether or not their skills match up with the skills required. Fortunately, one can learn new skills, but a match between what it takes and what is required is essential!

Second, the world is full of franchisees who settle for mediocrity and are okay with just "getting by." This attitude often leads to failure.

Third, some franchisees don't "own" their success or their failure for that matter. They play the "poor me" card and spend valuable time coming up with reasons why they are not successful. Many even blame it on the franchisor.

Fourth, many franchisees spend more time thinking and talking about what their business *could be* rather than spending their time and energy executing their plan and getting the job done.

Someone very wise captured the *"essence of survival"* in this very simple story. "Every day in Africa a gazelle wakes up. It knows it must run faster than the fastest lion or it will be killed. Every morning a lion wakes up. It knows it must outrun the slowest gazelle or it will starve to death. It doesn't matter whether you are a lion or a gazelle, when the sun comes up you'd better be running." This is a great principle for franchisees to live by.

If a successful franchisee needs this mentality just to survive, imagine the mentality one must have to really succeed and be outstanding! Alex Rodriquez, the highest paid major league baseball player ever, says it this way; "Hard work and sweat do not guarantee success, but without it, success is impossible. So enjoy your sweat!"

Studies of what it takes to succeed as a franchisee reveal that the sooner one accepts the fact that owning a business is tough, and truly succeeding at it is even tougher, the sooner the franchisee begins to take the steps to higher ground. Once you see it for what it is, you can turn your franchise business around if it needs it, or simply kick it up a notch and increase your sales and profitability. Our goal with this book is not just to help you be more successful, but also to help you ENJOY the sweat... ENJOY the process.

THE FORMULA FOR FRANCHISE SUCCESS

What is the formula for franchise success? Before I share it with you let me warn you that it takes several steps and it could take some attitude adjustments along the way. But, you obviously want help or you wouldn't be reading this book, so hang on and get ready to take your game to a whole new level.

The formula for franchise success includes these steps:

- Develop the proper "success" mindset
- Become a life long student of marketing and business development
- Own your success
- Accept Accountability
- Execute and TAKE ACTION

Let's explore these elements a bit deeper.

Develop the Proper "Success" Mindset

It's interesting the number of people I meet who either *want* to own their own business or *do* own their own business. The other interesting thing I see is this: out of those who own their own business, many seem to be run by it; meaning, their business runs their life. They don't seem to have much time for themselves or for their family. Instead of them owning the business, the business owns them. Many I run into are struggling and not enjoying it. Getting out of this rut starts with the first three steps in the formula.

First, begin with **visualizing, with absolute clarity, what you want**. I'll never forget the warm summer August evening kicking back on the grass counting the stars with my dad some 29 years ago. We had just come home from a ride in his brand new, fire-engine-red Porsche. I had expressed to my dad that I wanted one just like it some day. A discussion followed that has directed my life ever since. I asked him, "Dad? How can I be successful enough to be able to afford a nice sports car like this one day?" One of the main points of our discussion that night, when I was only 10 years old, is when he said, "You need to create a way to make money while you sleep. There are two ways to do that. One way is to invest your money into good investments so that it is earning you interest in your sleep, and the other way is to own your own business." So own my own business I would.

Second, **become a life long student of marketing, and business development**. Something I paid little attention to as I started and grew my first few businesses was just how hard it would be. WOW! It was tough! I thought it would be so much easier. Since then, from my own experience, and many interviews with successful franchisees, here is something I've learned: Starting and growing a business usually takes twice the money, three times longer than projected, and four times the amount of effort and stress one thinks it will. I have figured out since then that there are 3 types of people when it comes to learning from others:

1. This first type includes those with great big egos. They make mistakes and don't learn from them. This type of person is invincible and "knows everything."

2. The next type learns from their mistakes and tries to avoid making them again in the future.

3. The last type, and the wisest in my opinion, learns from others' mistakes and successes and uses that knowledge to capitalize on successes while minimizing mistakes. This type will, of course, still run across challenges on their own they didn't anticipate. However, the business person armed with knowledge of what works and what doesn't work will, in almost every case, be more successful.

Effective marketing can be the difference between having a decent franchise business and having an incredible franchise business. If you don't yet see marketing that way, hopefully, by reading this book and working through the exercises, you will. Actually, marketing can be one of the most enjoyable parts of your business, especially if your marketing efforts make your business more profitable. This means that, if you aren't already, you need to become a life long student of marketing and business development.

Third, **successful franchisees own their success**. In many cases, success boils down to the principles of responsibility and accountability and/or the lack of execution. For example, we live in a time where we know more about health and have more medical technology at our fingertips than ever before. We live in an age where study after study has proven that proper diet combined with exercise helps us become and stay leaner, healthier, and ultimately happier. Why then is more than 12 % of our GNP (Gross National Product) spent on health care? Why are there more sick Americans now than ever before? I would submit that it is due to the lack of execution, to not taking responsibility or accepting accountability for doing what we know we should do.

THE BUCK STOPS HERE

THE LAST TWO ELEMENTS of the franchise success formula are so important they will each be addressed in individual chapters. During those early years when I was drowning in my business and completely miserable, I was pointing fingers at everyone and everything I could think of:

Corporate: It was my franchisor's fault. After all, isn't their job to market my store?

Bad locations: I would have been successful had I been in better locations.

The weather: If only it were warmer or colder.

Not enough product offerings: Yes, that was it. Our menu was too limited.

Bad employees: It's tough to get good employees these days. It's their fault.

And the list didn't stop there! I would grab onto whatever excuse I could find until one day I learned the golden principle that helped me turn it around. It's called the accountability factor.

The Accountability Factor

I'm sure you've heard the phrase, "If it is going to be, it is up to me!" Well, in the franchise business, as in life, it is true! One of the biggest challenges in owning your own franchise business is feeling out of control. The extent to which we accept accountability determines the extent to which we are in control. And generally, those franchisees in control are usually more successful.

To illustrate I'd like to share a concept I learned from Dr. William Guillory, founder of Innovations International. I'll demonstrate the principle using 3 different individual franchise owner scenarios.

1. The first franchise owner wakes up daily with the mentality and mindset that his actions determine 50% of his success. The other 50% is up to fate and outside factors. The percentage that we are not in control determines to what extent we are the victim, or out of control. In this scenario, this particular owner has a 50% success rate that day, based on his attitude. Whether you agree or disagree, is it okay for this individual to attack his day and business like this? Sure it is. Basically, if he is 50% in control, 50% of his success is up to him and his actions. This person may look like this:

Accountability Factor

2. The second franchise owner determines that he and his actions determine 70% of his success in business. He is willing to accept that what he does and what he can control will make him in control 70% of the time. Now whether you agree or disagree, is it okay for this individual to attack his day and business like this? Sure it is. According to this individual, 70% of what he does will control his success and the other 30% is up to outside factors.

3. The third franchise owner determines that 100% of what happens in his life and in his business is due to him and his actions and 0% of his success or failure is determined by outside factors he cannot control. Now again, is it okay for this individual to attack his day and business like this? Sure it is. And, according to this individual, 100% of what he does will control his success and the other 0% is up to outside factors. This doesn't mean that outside conditions and factors won't come his way, it simply means he will approach EVERYTHING in his business as if it were up to HIM. This franchisee may look like this:

100% Responsible 100% Accountable

The Buck Stops Here

Regardless of outside conditions and things out of one's realm of control, assuming these three franchise owners consistently adopted this mentality, who would generally be in more control? Who would generally be more successful?

Where do you fall in the accountability factor? If you are not where you need to be, take action now and get there as quickly as possible.

EXECUTE AND TAKE ACTION!

THE FINAL ELEMENT in the franchise success formula is to **EXECUTE and TAKE ACTION.**

Marketing and Exercise

Have you ever tried a diet to shed some pounds? Let me guess what happened. In the beginning you were really committed. After a few days or a week you saw a few minor results, but you didn't see them quickly enough. What happened then? In many cases people get to this point, they get frustrated and give up saying, "Well, that diet didn't work!"

Or perhaps you were successful at sticking to a diet and exercise long enough to really make a difference. How did it feel? It felt great, didn't it? How about when you were exercising and you got your endorphins going. Wow!...talk about a great feeling, right? The first 10 minutes of exercising, on any given day, is always the toughest. But, about 10 minutes into it "BAM", the endorphins kick in and you are invincible! Think about it.

So what happens? Do you gain the weight back? If so why? Was it the diet's fault? Was it your personal trainer's fault? Was it the food's fault? In most cases, probably not. It is very likely that you got the results, got complacent, started backing off on the exercise, and slowly introduced unhealthy foods back into your diet. Let's not kid ourselves...it's tough, but if we stick with it we WILL get the results.

Nuts and Bolts

- There are many, many successful diet programs out there, but if you are not committed enough to actually do what you know you should do, you won't get the results. It's the same with success in your franchise business and in your marketing. You probably know much of what you SHOULD do but you simply don't do it, or at the very least, you don't do enough of it.

- Just like your body puts out endorphins, your marketing can feed you with "marketdorphins." Yes, I made that word up. But it's true. Once you have a little success in your business or your marketing how do you feel? It feels great right? The best time to make a sales call is always right after you've had a successful sales call. Why? Because of your marketdorphins. If you lack the marketing initiative, just get through the first 10 minutes, so to speak, until your marketdorphins kick in, and then keep the momentum going.

- If we eat the right foods we will be healthier. It's the same with marketing. The more of the RIGHT marketing we do, the more successful our business will be.

- And what about gaining the weight back? It has to do with complacency. Complacency will kill your health plan and it will absolutely kill your business. We must continue marketing constantly, just like we must eat properly and exercise constantly.

The same way taking action with the proper diet and exercise helps you get in better shape and enjoy better health, taking action and executing on your marketing plan will help your business get in better shape.

We have covered some of the key ingredients to be more successful as a franchisee. We have also determined that effective execution of marketing will take our business to the next level. Now it's time to discuss what marketing is and how to market more effectively.

Success Concept 7

GUERRILLA VS. TRADITIONAL MARKETING

BUSINESS THESE DAYS is all about business warfare. Let's face it. Your competition wants you out of the way. Your competition is going after your prospects and your customers. The challenge these days is that your competition may have a bigger budget than you do. They may run more ads in a year than you will ever run. Some of your competitors may have been around for years with a very loyal clientele. How do you overcome that?

The fact is, business is warfare and your competition is out to get you so you need to out-think and out-maneuver them at every turn. As we use the analogy of business warfare we will be using several words and terms that correlate with warfare such as strategies, tactics, weapons, etc. I would really like to point out though, that, in the spirit of guerrilla marketing, true guerrillas look for ways to work together whenever possible and promote strategic alliances to foster working in harmony.

Before we discuss what guerrilla marketing is let's first clarify what marketing is in general. You would be surprised to know how few people really understand.

Marketing is any contact that anyone or any part of your company has with anyone at anytime.

Let me repeat that. Marketing is any contact that anyone or any part of your company has with anyone at anytime. This includes letters, faxes, emails, packaging, envelopes, your receptionist, the cleanliness of your stores and the sales staff. Notice your company vehicles, your delivery staff, and anyone else that is ever in contact with any member of the public. Too often people think of marketing only as the coupon or ad that they send out or the television or radio commercial they produce. This is where the majority of companies really miss the boat. Marketing is every bit of contact any part of your company has with the public in any way.

Take a minute and think about your company right now. What image does your sign, your front door, or your website convey? Does it reflect what you would like it to? What about the person who answers the phone, your company's very first contact with the prospect? What about your letterhead or your business cards? What image does your lobby display? What about your store restrooms? Are they clean? Is everything orderly?

We did some consulting years ago with the Midas Muffler Company. One of the challenges they had was that they could only convert 70 percent of their inbound calls to appointments. In other words, only 7 out of 10 people that called for an appointment actually set an appointment. I'm sure that probably sounds okay but, think of the potential for growth from inbound calls. Could they make up the other thirty percent? What would it take? It was very interesting to find out. We listened for a short period of time and figured it out quite easily.

To the employees at Midas, the phone was an interruption in their day, an interruption. Isn't that interesting? People calling in for business were treated as an interruption. The closest person to the phone at the time happened to pick it up. That means the servicemen, sometimes the manager, but generally the service people, the mechanics. Their phone demeanor was absolutely atrocious. Not because they were not capable of doing a great job at it but because they had no formal training on phone answering. Plus, they were busy. They were doing the work. The phone calls were misunderstood. They did not see the calls as marketing but saw them as an *interruption* instead of the lifeblood of the company.

As part of our job to help them improve their sales and profits, we determined that the only person that should ever answer the phones should be either a person trained in converting calls to appointments or a fulltime receptionist. Most franchises of this sort cannot afford a fulltime receptionist and they share the responsibility. We understand this so the answer for Midas was for us to hold a half-day phone clinic. We repositioned the incoming calls to receive much more attention. People were not allowed to answer the phone unless they went through training. Within one week 94 percent of all incoming inquiries were converted into appointments. That's a 24% increase!

So how much did that actually cost the company? Not much at all. How hard was it? Not very hard. How much new profit was instantly added to the bottom line in this situation do you think? Quite a bit! Remember, marketing is any and all contact anyone in your company has with anyone at anytime. What then is Guerrilla Marketing?

What is Guerrilla Marketing?

Guerrilla Marketing is a collection of methods, weapons and strategies you can apply today to more effectively compete with large companies in business warfare. Where they have huge marketing budgets you will be using your imagination and your know-how. You will use your time effectively combined with low cost and no-cost marketing. **The goal of Guerrilla Marketing is to achieve the greatest amount of profits with the least investment possible.**

To explain this in more detail we will explore 19 ways guerrilla marketing differs from traditional marketing.

19 Ways Guerrilla Marketing Differs From Traditional Marketing

1. Instead of investing money in the marketing process, you will invest in four different areas: 1) **Time, 2) Energy, 3) Imagination, and 4) Knowledge.** For the past 2 years, every time I pick up my dry cleaning at Continental Cleaners, there has been a postcard size advertisement for Hot Realty attached to it. No kidding, every time. I have received nine of these same postcards. How much more effective is that than mailing them to me! Chances are, if those postcards were mailed to my home, I would hardly have noticed. But by using some time, energy, and imagination Hot Realty has captured my attention.

2. Instead of using guesswork, guerrilla marketing uses the **science of psychology** and the **laws of human behavior.** In other words, "Why is it that people buy?" Did you know that most buying decisions are made in the unconscious mind? People do not, as some may think, consciously select a brand to purchase. Instead, the unconscious mind, that inner, deeper portion that comprises 90 percent of a person's brainpower, figures out what brand one should purchase. It then sends a message to the conscious mind.

   Knowing this, it is also important to know that there are two ways to access the unconscious mind. One is by hypnosis and the other way is through repetition. Although hypnosis would be an interesting option, it is not possible. Studies have proven that through **repetition, repetition,**

repetition you will get into the unconscious mind of your prospects. Advertising leaders have frequently made the same point. The critical step now is for you to apply this new awareness to your future marketing. You will see it work.

3. **Profits** are the only yardstick you use to measure your marketing. Don't just count traffic, gross sales, or even the response to your ads. In my early years in business as a Jamba Juice Franchisee, I set out to lead the company in the sales increase category. At that time there were approximately 400 locations in 19 states. Two out of the five stores that I owned ended up being in the top five for growth in the company. I was so excited. We put out a ton of money in marketing and we were up in that top five. We gave out tons of coupons, spent a lot of money, and sold a lot of discounted product. We were exhausted by the end of that year.

   As I sat with my partner to look over our profits for that incredible sales year, I was absolutely dumbfounded to see that our net profit was barely above the prior year. How could that be? I was shocked! I was anticipating a great meeting to share these numbers. What a letdown. At that time we measured success by our gross sales and the traffic in our stores. I learned this: profits are the only yardstick you should use in measuring your marketing. The following year was much more profitable as our focus was turned to profit *not* just store traffic.

4. Guerrilla marketing is geared towards **small and medium size franchisees**, not businesses with unlimited bank accounts. However, you would be amazed at how many Fortune 500 companies are resorting to guerrilla mar-

keting. Many have figured out that the tools used here are extremely effective and generate more profits.

5. Guerrilla marketing emphasizes and practices fervent devotion to **customer follow-up**. Let's not forget about a customer once they have purchased. How much are your customers worth to you? How much does it cost you to gain a new customer? Do you know? Have you ever figured it out? If not, I suggest you go through that exercise. When you realize how much your customers are worth, you will try even harder to keep them for life. It costs so much less to hold on to a customer and enjoy their repeat business than to gain a new one. Yet so many companies go after the new ones, forgetting about their current customers.

We figured out in our Jamba Juice business that on average, on an annual basis, our customers spent about $412.00 per year. Our smoothies sold for $4.00 a piece. An average Jamba Juice customer drinks two smoothies a week. That is a lot of smoothies! If we did not follow up with our customers and treat them right, it was not a loss of just $4.00, it was a loss of $412.00 a year for many years to come. How much are your customers worth and are you investing enough time in following up with them? 68 percent of all business lost in the United States is due to a lack of follow up. Effective marketers follow up consistently and constantly.

6. **Guerrilla marketing makes marketing less intimidating**. Instead of intimidating small business owners, guerrilla marketing defines the marketing process and clarifies it. You can compete in the age where money often buys clients. Even with less spending you can be successful. Very often, it is truly the principle that, "It's the little

things in life that matter most." Guerrilla marketing capitalizes on the little things. Once you understand the marketing process and why people buy, marketing is not intimidating.

7. Instead of competing with other businesses, guerrilla marketing teaches **cooperation**. Go out of your way to help others and let them help you. This is often referred to as fusion marketing or co-op marketing. It is becoming very acceptable these days. How many commercials have you seen that, at the beginning, you think it is an ad for Coca-Cola and then halfway through you realize it is actually an ad for McDonald's? Wait, no, it's actually an ad for Disney's Finding Nemo movie. Well, actually it's an ad for all three. Although this is being done all the time with large companies, franchises can do it on a local level as well.

   Share a direct mail piece with a company that compliments yours and split the cost. Put brochures or coupons for other businesses in your bags or on your web site while those businesses do the same for you. Share mailing lists with other companies or have companies mail a letter to their customers or clients on your behalf, as you do the same for them. Help others and they will help you. Figure out what company you can team up with. Who would have thought that a real estate company would team up with a dry cleaner? Get creative. Who can you team up with?

8. Guerrillas are dedicated to **developing relationships**. Long-term relationships are paramount in the 21st Century. Most prospects need to be marketed to and want to develop a relationship before buying from you. Find ways to give your prospects useful information that will build

your relationship with them. If you have a website, offer a free download of information that they may find useful. Do you have a newsletter you can send them monthly or quarterly? Can you send a coupon for a free sample of your food, product, or service? Once people buy from you, how do you follow up with them? Do you send a thank you note? Do you send birthday cards? Remember, with most purchases, people will buy from you again and again if you have a good relationship with them.

9. Instead of believing that single marketing weapons work, such as advertising, guerrillas know that **only marketing combinations work**. Very often, too often really, we see businesses fail because they only use one or two marketing tools. Using a combination of many and varied marketing weapons at a time is needed to really be effective.

10. A tenth way guerrilla marketing differs from traditional marketing is that instead of growing linearly by adding new customers one at a time, guerrilla marketing suggests that you **grow geometrically** by enlarging each transaction. Go for more repeat sales and adding new customers. Here's an example, do you have products that you can add on to the sale? If you go to McDonald's and order a burger, what do you always get asked? "Would you like fries with that?" or "Would you like to make that a combo meal?" If you say yes to the combo meal, what do you get asked next? That's right. "Would you like to super size that today, sir?" Very tempting! It just is not by chance that you get asked those questions at McDonald's. They have a system in place to ensure every customer is asked those two questions. What about you? In your business, do you have a system to follow up with additional selling to your current customers?

11. Instead of growing with the idea of diversifying, Guerrilla Marketing suggests that you grow, but be sure to **maintain your focus**. Were you around when Coke decided to launch a wine product? It didn't last very long. Coke thought that since they had the corner on the cola market they could do the same with wine. Unfortunately for Coke, that idea flopped and cost them 89 million dollars. Gerber Baby Food decided to do the same and expand with a furniture and baby clothes line. It seemed to make sense at the time. But, it also faired poorly and lost the company 29 million dollars. Don't make a mistake and think that diversifying away from your main product is increasing your excellence. Have you been to In and Out Burger lately? I love that place. Have you tried their new pizza? Me either. They don't sell pizza, just awesome burgers, fries, and shakes. They get it and they are making a ton of money while focusing on what they do best. Make sure you do not diversify unless it makes sense.

12. Don't just aim your message at groups. Guerrilla marketing encourages you to **aim at individuals**. Traditional marketing calculates CPM or cost per thousand prospects. Guerrilla marketing counts CPP, or the cost per prospect. Figure out as much as you can about your customers. Why is it that they buy? Where do they hang out? What do they do with their spare time? Then target your marketing at those individuals who enjoy the same interests and activities as your customers do.

    Target marketing is much more effective than nontargeted marking because you can speak more personally to your prospects and it also lends to credibility, which is one of the reasons people buy. For example, one real estate agent may specialize in expensive homes over $750,000.00 in the ski areas of Colorado. Another agent may specialize in starter homes that cost less than $125,000.00. Get the idea? Target your marketing. Find your niche and set the target.

13. As well as counting up sales at the end of each month, guerrillas **count up new relationships**. They know that those relationships are the foundation of increased sales. Do not get caught up in the numbers as much as getting caught up in how many relationships you start.

14. Guerrillas think of what they **can give to a prospect**. Give prospects as much information as possible to make decisions. With internet technology you can really leverage your web site and offer free newsletters to communicate with and build relationships with your prospects. I know a chiropractor that had a yellow page ad that gave you a report on how to choose a chiropractor. The ad did not try to sell people. It offered what many people were already thinking. The ad addressed that feeling of, "Hey! This is overwhelming trying to choose a chiropractor" by sharing useful information to help you decide. This woman was a true Guerrilla and is very successful. Another example is for an air conditioning or heating company to offer an article or brochure on how to reduce your utility bill.

15. **Don't avoid technology,** embrace it. If you are techno-phobic, then make an appointment with a techno shrink. Technophobia is fatal these days. We have worked with a particular client for years. He is the highest volume mattress retailer in the Bay Area in San Francisco specializing in very expensive mattresses. Years ago when the internet came out he was already very successful. His younger

employees tried for years and years to get him to use a web site. He finally buckled under the pressure, not thinking it would do much for his business. Today he receives more leads from his web site than any other sources. The lesson? If you are not computer savvy or web savvy, get somebody that is, because you need to be on the web.

16. **All guerrilla marketing is intentional**. We monitor the whole package. Think of Disneyland on this one. Everything Disney does is intentional. They are marketing geniuses; from the parking lot to the parade, rides, Mickey and all. You are engulfed in "Disney Mania" for the entire experience. Ever wear those Mickey Mouse ears you bought, and wore, all through Disneyland? From the French fry shapes to the lollipop you buy, everything is Disney.

There was a furniture company that had 16 locations but did less volume than their smaller competitor. The owners of the store decided to check out why they were getting crushed by their competition. They found 38 levels of detail in the sales process from when a prospect walked in the door to how their furniture was delivered. They did 38 little things right every day. That is what it takes these days. How much attention do you pay to detail in your sales process? Pay attention and do a lot of things right every day.

17. Gain consent from people before sending your marketing materials. This is called **permission marketing**. There is a youth camp in the State of New York. It is the most successful camp in the state and also the most expensive. They run a little ad in the camping directory to send for a free video about camp. They have a booth at the camping trade shows. The goal of the video is to get the people

interested in having an in-home consultation. The sales people then go to the home to give a great presentation. 84 percent of the people who have the in-home presentation sign their kids up for the camp.

In some cases it is easier to get prospects to take small steps toward a big purchase. This camp would not have near the success if they simply ran an ad with the tuition cost in hopes that people would buy. Get permission to market to your prospects especially if you are selling a big-ticket item.

18. Instead of being a monologue with one party doing all the communicating, **Guerrilla Marketing is a dialogue** with both parties communicating interactively. Ask, then listen. Let the prospect tell you what he needs. If you offer a solution to what he needs, you will make a sale and gain a customer. Talk to your customers about specific things you can do to add to their customer experience.

19. Guerrilla marketing provides you with **more than 100 marketing weapons** and advertising is only one of them! Get ready to arm yourself with knowledge.

BENEFITS, ADVANTAGES AND TARGET MARKETS

THIS SECTION OF THE BOOK focuses on the benefits of doing business with you. There is absolutely no mystery about why guerrillas prevail and others fall by the wayside. They know *when* to *launch* a marketing attack, how long to *continue* it, and *how* to do it. They know which battles are worth going after and which are not. They have learned how to win. They know that <u>*marketing is a process*</u>, not just an event. They know their products and why people do business with them. That is especially important to know prior to creating marketing materials.

It is critical to determine the benefits of doing business with you and your company. This is an extremely important list so don't be shy or modest with this list. Be sure to list every possible benefit you can think of no matter how minor it might seem. This is your opportunity to boast about what makes you and your product so great.

You may want to call a meeting, invite your key personnel and at least one customer to this meeting. The sole purpose of this gathering is to come up with a list of benefits that you and your company offer, and yes, you probably have to bring in some doughnuts and juice or lunch to make it a great meeting. The reason you invite a customer is so that you find out from them what they recognize your benefits to be. You may learn that the customer perceives value that you don't realize as such.

For example, one day I asked my wife why she goes into Big Apple Bagels for her daily Diet Coke when she can get it more conveniently at the corner gas station for less money. She replied, "Because of the ice." "The ice?" I said. "Yeah, they have hospital ice." "What is hospital ice?" I asked. Come on now, ice is ice, or so I thought. I guess hospital ice is softer or something of that nature. Well, I doubt that on Big Apple Bagel Company's *"benefits of doing business with us list"* they have identified hospital ice. This just goes to show you could be amazed at why people really do business with you.

Just yesterday I saw a U-Haul moving truck. They know one of the reasons people use their trucks is because they have lower loading decks than most of their competition. Next time you look at the back of a U-Haul truck, look at how they have huge arrows pointing to how low the deck is and you will see the statement, "Our lower loading decks make your mover EASIER!"

Something to keep in mind here is your franchise company and brand has its own benefits. You and your particular locations may have some others to add upon it. For example, your particular location may have a drive through while others don't. Capitalize on it. Your particular branch may have a certain type of technology better than the average franchises out there. Your particular location may be better at providing customer service. So be thinking not only of the benefits the franchise has but also you individually.

Once you know WHY people do business with you, you can really highlight it in your marketing. This can be very effective at driving up your profits. Why do people do business with you? Let's get busy. Take some time with this and get on with the list of benefits of doing business with you. You may come up with more than ten or less than ten, but really dig here and put the necessary time into it. The key here is once you have identified them, use them and highlight them in your marketing.

EXECUTE and TAKE ACTION!

The Benefits of Doing Business with _____

_____

_____

_____

_____

_____

_____

_____

_____

_____

_____

Your Competitive Advantages

Hopefully your eyes were open to some benefits you were not sure you actually offered. Now we are going to talk about your competitive advantages. As you select your competitive advantages understand that this is where you are going to be hanging your marketing hat. Competitive advantages are those things that set you apart from the competition. It is what makes you unique. I live in Phoenix, Arizona, as I have mentioned before. If you have ever been there you probably observed a few things. Number one, if you were there in the middle of summer you realized it is about the hottest place on the planet. It really is.

Number two, it is a huge place. It goes on forever and ever and happens to be one of the fastest growing cities in America with over four million people already in 2005. Thirdly, it is retail center heaven.

There are more small retail centers in Phoenix than anywhere I have ever been. There are shops on almost every corner. It is unbelievable. You can find almost every brand in America in Phoenix. As a consumer it is great because there is so much to choose from. When it comes to food choices alone, we have so many food choices in each food category it is almost impossible to choose.

If you want Asian food you can choose from Tokyo Express, Shogun Express, Oriental Express, Kyoto Bowl, New China Buffet, China Palace, Little Tokyo, Shanghai Club, Bamboo Grove, etc. For Mexican food and the fast food category alone you have Del Taco and Taco Bell, but also, Alberto's, Filberto's, Umberto's, Baja Fresh, Chipotle, etc. Get the picture? It is a consumer's paradise, but what about from a seller's perspective? In today's world consumers have so many companies to choose from that it makes it very difficult to compete.

These days so many people want to own their own business. One of the best things about this great country of ours, obviously, is free enterprise. But with free enterprise comes competition. With free enterprise comes the necessity to compete or your company will die. What is it that sets your franchise company apart? Not just the franchise, but your particular store, branch, office, etc.? Out of all the companies out there, why would I, as a consumer, choose you and your company?

Each of us, as consumers, is inundated every day with thousands of decisions to make. You know, centuries ago the cave men went out to hunt for dinner. The meat choices were very scarce. They ate what they could kill that happened to live in their geographic area. They ate the fruits and vegetables that grew in their region. Today however, when we hunt for dinner we have so much to choose from: red meat, white meat, fish, pork, etc. Then we need to decide if we want breast, loin, rump, leg, or cutlet. Do we prefer it fresh, frozen, canned, or preserved? Which store should we go to? Which meat do we buy? Is Rancher's Reserve, Black Angus,

USDA Approved, or the one on sale better? That is just the meat department. We have had an explosion of choice in almost every area of our life.

In the area of cars, we used to choose from Ford, GM, Chrysler, or American Motors with only those few different vehicle models available. In today's environment we have hundreds of vehicle models available from many different manufacturers including Ford, GM, Toyota, Chrysler, Honda, Suzuki, Isuzu, Mazda, Mitsubishi, BMW, Porsche, Fiat, Kia, Volvo, Mercedes, Ferrari, Lamborghini, and the list goes on. Then of course we have our choice of tires from ten or more large manufacturers.

And what about electronics? Speaking of our choices in television and radio, just a few decades ago there existed three major television networks. Now with cable television an average consumer with a basic package can access over 150 channels any time of the day or night. And computers? With computers and the invention of the internet we can access information like never before. We no longer have to leave the house to shop. We shop all over the world with a stroke of a few buttons with the use of the internet.

We live and compete in a cruel competitive world, folks. Mediocrity is not good enough. In fact, in most situations, *good* is not enough. We must be *great*. We must differentiate ourselves from others. So what are your competitive advantages? What is it that makes your product or your company better than your competition?

The concept of being unique or different is so important and relevant today. Not only because there is more competition but also because the competition is tougher and smarter than ever before. We must be unique and differentiate ourselves and our products from our competitors.

Let me share with you a few examples of competitive advantages. For instance, the company, Avis, has a slogan, "We Try Harder." The company slogans for McDonald's, at least lately are, "We Love to See Your Smile" and "I'm Lovin' It!" Jack in the Box, "We do not make your meal until you order it." Baja Fresh, "Every order is made fresh, no microwaves or cans." At Nordstrom they will take anything back. Wal-Mart is known for being a great value with, "Always low prices. Always!" AM/PM Gasoline is generally the cheapest. Costco is known for both food and products at a cheaper price. Cadillac automobiles specialize in expensive quality and luxury. Hyundai automobiles are a good value. Southwest Airlines, best value air travel. American Airlines, specializes in business travelers. Get the idea?

You need to decide what your competitive advantages are because there are so many companies out there that have competitive advantages. Another example is Splenda. The sweetener has made a huge dent in the artificial sugar market. It has differentiated itself by positioning itself as the sweetener that tastes like sugar because it is made from real sugar. But it contains no NutraSweet which people have become very concerned about. This has given Splenda over 50 percent of the market share in the sweetener category in a very short period of time.

Another example of differentiating is Starbucks Coffee. Starbucks' clientele frequents them for several reasons. Is the coffee really that much better than anywhere else? No. It is very good coffee but most people go there for the atmosphere and the prestige that goes along with Starbucks. The atmosphere in each Starbucks location defines them. It is warm and sophisticated. For some reason a person just feels sophisticated as they enter a Starbucks lobby. Do you not?

Aside from the warm, fine, sophisticated environment and the imported coffee beans from Guatemala and the high hills of Colombia, Starbucks is widely known for their service. As you come to the counter you will receive a "Hi, welcome to Starbucks. What can I get for you?" delivered with a warm smile. I see a "Now

Hiring" sign in their window. It really speaks to why they have such phenomenal service. The sign is so nice it almost looks like a nice piece of art on the wall. As you look more closely you notice that it is a picture of many green apron strings dangling against a nice mocha colored background and it says, "We are known for our coffee, but our people make us famous. Join our team. Apply today. Create the experience. starbucks.com." That's classy! But notice too that Starbucks differentiates itself in several ways, through the environment, the people who work there, and the service they offer.

Of course you realize that many of your competitors offer the same benefits you listed in the previous exercise. However, you also offer some benefits that they do not. These unique benefits are your competitive advantages and the ones you need to focus on. Do not underestimate the power of pointing out what you think is the obvious. For example, a pizza joint may say on their marketing material, "Dough made fresh daily." Is not most pizza dough made fresh daily? I think it is but no one points that out.

Baja Fresh (fresh mex) is another example. They point out that they do not use microwaves or food out of cans. The fact is, there are probably other fresh mex places that don't either, but Baja Fresh points it out. So it is important to take some time and look for the obvious and the not so obvious in your business. Could it be a competitive advantage? Select your competitive advantages from the benefits list that you just created.

Are you getting the idea? What are the things that give you and your company and your products a competitive advantage? Take time now to list your competitive advantages. Remember, don't just list what sets your franchise apart, but also what sets you apart from the rest in your particular branch or location.

EXECUTE and TAKE ACTION!

List your competitive advantages here.

The Competitive Advantages of _____

_____

_____

_____

_____

_____

_____

_____

_____

_____

_____

_____

_____

_____

_____

_____

_____

_____

Your Target Market

Everything we've done so far has lead us to the important discussion of target markets. Before selecting marketing methods remember this important principle: *it is not necessary to say everything to everybody, nor is it possible.* If you try saying everything to everybody, you'll end up saying everything to nobody or nothing to everybody. What a mouthful. Instead, you should strive to say something to somebody. Your marketing message is the something. Your target audience is the "somebody."

Just as you take care in selecting what you will say, you should take equal care in selecting to whom it will be said. It is not acceptable to say the right thing to the wrong people. The more specifically you can target your marketing, the more profits you will earn. And this is the good news, you may have one target market, but in all likelihood, you may have several. The more targets you have, the more bull's-eyes you can score. Use geographical, demographic and psychographic criteria to define your markets. The more defined your target market, the easier your marketing becomes.

EXECUTE and TAKE ACTION!

Now take time and list your primary and your secondary target markets on the space provided.

Primary Target Market of _____

_____

_____

_____

_____

Secondary Target Market of _____

_____

_____

_____

_____

BUILDING CONSENT WITH SOFT STEPS

REMEMBER, guerrilla marketing is all about creating and maintaining relationships. So how do we build relationships? By creating a series of soft steps. You can build trust, gain rapport, and gain consent for soft steps which eventually lead to the hard step of buying. Examples of soft steps would be: free brochures, consultations, demonstrations, tours, samples, videos, audio tapes, booklets, estimates, seminars, newsletters, parties, special events, appraisals, etc.

Once you make a sale, you continue with more after-sale soft steps that encourage your customers to remain loyal and make repeat purchases. That's what it's all about, right? Business would be a breeze and guerrillas could devote their talents elsewhere if customers walked right in and handed over the money. But we know that business doesn't even pretend to be a breeze and we know that guerrillas have got to give their company all they've got before any customer walks in and hands anybody any money.

For the customer, handing their money over to you in the form of a check, credit card, cash, purchase order, etc. can be a really hard step to take sometimes. It is one not taken lightly and in many cases, it is one not taken at all. But, the guerrilla doesn't just sit there during that all-important selection process. The successful franchisee gets involved in it. Successful franchisees make it simple to take the hard step of buying. They accomplish that by offering soft steps that can be taken prior to the hard step. They help customers make their selection. You can make a customer feel comfortable with information, with service and with your caring attitude. A list of soft steps is coming up in just a moment.

All of the soft steps make it extremely easy to take that hard step. In fact, it doesn't even seem hard anymore because prospects have been working their way toward it; guided by you, step by step, with your sense of the marketing. In every sales situation there is a hard step; so it stands to reason that in most sales situations there are also several soft steps or at least one. There is no evidence that the quantity of soft steps affects profitability but ample data supports the premise that *quality* soft steps can increase profits.

Every successful franchisee knows that before a sale is made, momentum must be created. One of the most valuable ways to create momentum is to get customers to say "yes." This is the underlying force behind soft steps. For example, "Do you want our free video brochure?" "Yes." "Would you like a free sample?" "Yes." "Are you looking for a 24-hour-a-day plumber?" "Yes." So what exactly are soft steps? They are different from bribes because they are far more than a free gift. They are a direct introduction to your products or services. They are marketing weapons that create the momentum that leads to the hard step.

Nuts and Bolts - 10 Examples of Soft Steps

1. An offer of a free sample

2. An offer of a free demonstration

3. An offer of a free brochure

4. An offer of a free video tape

5. An offer of a free audio tape

6. An offer of a free consultation

7. An offer of a free booklet

8. An offer of a free estimate

9. An offer to attend a free seminar

10. An offer of a free newsletter

Have we left any out? You bet. This is where you continue the list as it pertains to your specific business. The best soft steps I've seen combine awareness gained through media exposure with the offer of a free brochure and a free consultation. That's three soft steps and it's usually enough. Just ten years ago, one step, the hard step, may have been enough. But, when you're in the middle of an information age, you've just got to be prepared to offer information to people who justifiably ask for it.

Mark Shawver of Pizza Pan gets this concept. He just brought the Pizza Pan franchise to California. Most people in California haven't heard of them yet. They have a great offer, it's continually "Buy 1 get 2 Free." Not only that, but they have an extensive menu offering from ribs to many types of buffalo wings and much more. So he has a banner that says "Free Samples." Every customer that comes in gets a free sample, not necessarily the pizza, because it's a pizza joint. He offers ribs, wings, and the other unique items from the menu people wouldn't think of ordering. Mark's business has dramatically increased since he implemented this one small, yet powerful soft step.

EXECUTE and TAKE ACTION!

List examples of "soft steps" you can use in your particular business

_____

_____

_____

_____

_____

_____

_____

_____

_____

Now I invite you to go back and prioritize them and begin putting them to use.

Success Concept 10

WHY PEOPLE ACTUALLY BUY

TO UNDERSTAND HOW to best sell your product or service, we first need to understand why people buy. Think for a minute about something you purchased in the past week. This could be something as simple as ordering a pizza for dinner or as complex as buying a new car—anything. Why did you buy it? Why did you choose that particular pizza place? Was it because you had a coupon, or is it because it's the best pizza in town? If you purchased a car recently, why did you choose that particular one? Was it because of how it makes you feel when you drive it, or because of its safety rating? People buy for many different reasons. Once we decide why people buy your particular product or service, it will be easier for you to target your marketing to them; thus making your marketing more effective.

People buy:

- *Promises you make.*

- *Your **credibility**.* Credibility is built through repetition, repetition, repetition and fulfilling promises that you make.

- *Solutions to their problems.*

- *You, your employees, your service department, etc.*

Everything about your product, store, website, or company's reputation can be solid, but one or two bad employees can blow the whole thing apart. Let me give you an example. I entered into a sandwich shop the other day, the name of which I will keep anony-mous. Two employees were talking. I got no greeting whatsoever. I looked at the young lady standing there and she looked back at me with absolutely zero expression. I looked over at the man baking bread and I later found out that he was the owner of the place. I got no acknowledgement from him either. So I looked back at the young lady. Her face was still cold as ice. So I decided to make a game out of this thing. I wanted to be greeted. So finally I greeted her with an enthusiastic, "So how you doing tonight?" She nearly rolled her eyes with the look of being bothered. "Fine. Can I get you something?"

I never returned to that place. A new sandwich shop opened up right across the street a few months later. You know, it is 20 percent more expensive, but I get greeted there every time and it is now the only sandwich shop I go to. Remember, marketing is every bit of contact that you have with every single person and so it needs to be communicated properly. One employee can blow it for your entire company like it did for the first sandwich shop.

People also buy:

- *Wealth, safety, success, security, love, and acceptance.* Tap into these human emotions in your marketing.

- *Freedom from risk granted by your warranty and guarantee.*

    Do you have one? Is it strong?

- *Your reputation, your company's reputation, your products' rep-utation and they buy a good name.* Do not let your employees ruin it for you. Get the right people working for you that will represent your company and your product the way you want it represented.

- *Other people's opinions about your business.* A few months ago I was in the process of purchasing a swimming pool. I talked to many people that had pools to find a reputable company. After all, that is what we do, don't we? We talk to people about things that they have purchased. "Where did you go?" "How was it?" "What was the experience like?" "Are you happy?" After all, it was a large purchase and I wanted to find out who my friends trusted.

Six pool companies were mentioned among the friends that I talked to and not one of our friends were happy with even one of the pool builders in Arizona that they had used. The reasons varied, but most of it came down to their follow up or lack thereof with fixing problems that they, the pool company, were responsible for. We finally went with a small, less expensive company because we figured it was worth a gamble. Most likely we would have problems with them so we might as well save some money in doing so. Sadly enough we are barely into the process and are already less than impressed. Sadly for them, we have already had several people ask us if we would recommend them. I'm sure you can guess what our answer was.

- *Expectations based upon your marketing.* Make sure that you set realistic expectations so your customers will not be let down once they purchase your product. Keep in mind, your first sale to a customer is only the beginning of your relationship. Happy customers buy for years and years following the first sale. Too many companies forget this and that is your opportunity to service those people.

- *Hope for their own and for their company's future.* Years ago I owned a business that had a huge cash flow problem. I had to infuse new capital several times just to make the payroll. I was sick to my stomach every day. I did not sleep at night. I was sinking into a deep depression. It was miserable and I do not like to look back on it. I did not even want to wake up in the morning because I knew that I had to face the people I owed money to, not to mention my partner that I reassured so many times, "I swear it will pay off. We just need a little more money and a little more time."

On one particularly rough day I got a call from a business consulting company. They mentioned that they could help me with my cash flow problems. Ding, ding, ding, ding. That was a hot button for me at that time. I set the appointment. The guy flew in from out of town to meet me. Here is the interesting part. Somehow this guy got me to commit to an enormous amount of money for an eight week consulting agreement. I am talking a lot of money here. But he sold me on the hope for my future, hope for the success of my company. So he got the contract. I got the cash flow problem straightened out and miraculously had the money to pay for it and turned that business into a thriving success. Remember, people buy hope for their own or their company's future. Give them that hope.

- *Brand names over strange names.* Do everything you can to build your brand. You do not have to be in business for 20 or 30 years to develop a brand. Just be consistent and aggressive in your niche market and you will build your brand.

- *Consistency they see you exhibit.* I recently bought a new house. I needed a loan. I had a great real estate agent, Angie Simon with Phantom Realty. She was a great friend and sold a lot of houses. We hired her. I bought her consistency because I have seen it before.

Angie referred me to Tom, my mortgage guy. In our first meeting with Tom, my wife and I told him we had never used the same mortgage person twice because every previous one had over-promised and under-delivered. They promised it would be seven to ten days from start to finish. Not only did they fall short of their commitment, they didn't communicate with me during or after the loan process. I want to be communicated with.

Tom leaned forward and reassured us he called his clients weekly to update them on the process. Tom called weekly for the next three weeks. I loved it. This guy was really following through with his commitment. Every Tuesday afternoon, like clockwork, he called. Wow! This was great.

During the process we told Tom that we wanted to get a pool. We asked about adding it to the mortgage. The answer was no but Tom had an idea. He suggested we take out a home equity loan the day after closing to secure the needed funds for a pool and the fix-up list.

Angie, our real estate agent, sent us a great gift basket to follow up and thank us. Not only did she send us a great gift basket, but she followed up for the next three days making sure that everything was just great with our new house and we got a $500.00 gift certificate from the real estate company towards some new furniture at a local Robb and Stucky furniture store. I was overwhelmed. I have never received this from a real estate agent before. It was great.

And where is Tom? I have not talked to Tom since three days before we closed on the house. He knew I needed more money and that I wanted to get it done right after the purchase. It has been five weeks and no word from Tom. Where is the thank you from Tom?

We ordered the pool and I need cash right now. Tom doesn't get it. There is money sitting on the table for him and he's not going to get it because he hasn't followed up or followed through. Doesn't he know that people move, on average, every four years in Arizona? Sadly enough, a fifty cent thank you card would have kept me happy. Consistency is key!

And they buy:

- *The professionalism of your marketing materials.* Do your marketing materials demonstrate the level of professionalism that you would like? Make sure that they do.

- *Value*, which is not necessarily the same thing as price. Make sure you realize the difference.

- *Selection.* Do you have enough of a good selection for people to choose from? Do you let them know about that selection through free sampling etc.?

- *Convenience.* Are you convenient enough for your customers? We live in a 24/7 society. Are you and your company convenient enough for your customers every single day, 24 hours a day? Take a look at your hours if you have a storefront. If you are online, that is great because people will buy at crazy hours of the night.

- *Your identity* as conveyed in your marketing. What exactly is your company's identity? What is it that you want people to think of and feel when they think of your company?

- *Neatness and cleanliness.* While conducting research for a restaurant about why their customers chose them over others we learned something very interesting. It was amazing to learn how many people mentioned clean restrooms as one of the reasons they liked the restaurant. Do you know people like that? Maybe you are like that. They figure if the company cares enough about the detailed cleaning of the restroom then they must really care about the details in the kitchen. It makes sense.

And don't think clean restrooms are only important for restaurants. I had a guy, a man mind you, say he passes three or four gas stations on the way to and from work, but always goes to the one furthest away because it has clean restrooms. This is a guy. I didn't think men cared about that kind of thing, but they do. Are you kidding me? Aren't you going there for the gas and perhaps some convenience food? To a lot of people, clean restrooms make the difference. People buy neatness and cleanliness. How clean is your establishment?

- *Easy access to information you offer on your website.* In this day and age where there is so much information available, people do not want difficulty finding information about you. Make it simple for them. Give them access to as much information as you can for free. People love information.

- *Honesty.* Let's be honest. If you and your product cannot give something the prospect wants, be honest about it. We live in an age of great skepticism. True guerrillas are known for their honesty.

- *Success.* Your success can fit with their success. I am talking about genuine success. People generally want to do business with successful companies and successful individuals.

- *Good taste* and they know good taste from bad taste. Get to know your prospects and how they define good taste. I will never forget the experience I had that went from good to sour at Bell Ford in Arizona. We had purchased a car from them several years ago. The salesman, Joe Corella, was great. I loved the guy. He was honest and very likeable. He really took care of us and our kids every time we went in.

We had to return a few days after the purchase to trade for a different model that was not available at the original purchase. My wife and I were there with our kids. My 12-

year-old was at the table with us and the sales manager ended up taking care of us because Joe was out for some reason or another. We got handed off to the sales manager. No big deal, I thought.

My 12-year-old was sitting at the table with us when the sales manager started using profanity, obviously thinking he was being funny. It was inappropriate language period, but especially in front of my wife and my 12-year-old son. It was very uncomfortable and in very poor taste. I know he was trying to be funny, but he was not. He was actually quite offensive. I left with a poor taste in my mouth. Know how your prospects and customers define good taste and then appeal to it.

- *Instant gratification*, like I needed when my air conditioner failed in 115-degree weather. I needed something right then and right there, and luckily I got it. I used the first company that could get to my house.

- *Confidence*. The confidence you display in your business and in your products.

Of course, not everyone buys for the same reason. That's why it's important to appeal to as many of these emotional reasons as possible and to integrate them into your marketing. I am always amazed at how many ads I see every day that tell only the company name, address, phone number, and perhaps what they do, but they are really missing the boat. Remember, solve problems for people and use these reasons people buy in your marketing. You will see more profits.

YOUR 7-STEP MARKETING PLAN

LET'S TALK ABOUT the seven steps of writing your effective marketing plan, the key word being *effective*. This is where the rubber meets the road. This is where it all starts to come together so you can achieve more profits. To begin talking about marketing plans we find that generally franchisees fall into one of the following categories:

1. Some have a marketing plan but it is so big and complex that it sits on the shelf because nobody in the company understands it except the person who wrote it. Have you seen those things before? They are like the Encyclopedia Britannica. They are impressive to look at for sure, yet, they are often too hard to understand, let alone to implement. This is crazy and it is extremely counter-productive. One franchise business puts out, from their corporate office, a new marketing plan guide every two years. These things are beautiful, but not even a little bit practical or useable. The point being, make sure you develop a marketing plan that is simple, straightforward, and easy to use. Keep reading for details on how.

2. Perhaps you fall into the second category. Your plan is that you do not have any plan at all and you just wing it. Is this you or have you done that before? Believe it or not, *most* businesses fall into this category. The business

owner uses whatever advertising happens to be in front of her at that time. These people make emotional decisions when it comes to marketing, like the Val Pak or Money Mailer, or sometimes the ADVO sales rep happens to catch you on a tough day for sales, so you might go with that. This is called "reactive marketing" versus "proactive marketing." Not good. We find that most franchisees use the marketing weapons that are marketed to them the most. Please be careful with this. It is very dangerous. It is like going to the grocery store when you are starving. Have you ever done that before? You end up buying all sorts of food you do not need and generally very fattening, sugary foods at that.

3. Perhaps this third category describes you better: you have a plan and you use it occasionally when you feel like it, when you happen to be in the mood. Or, you use it sporadically, one month on, one month off. Is this you? If it is, I invite you to change. It is crucial to be consistent. Create your plan and use it consistently.

4. Hopefully this fourth category is your category: you have a plan and use it continually. If this is you, excellent work! Keep it up.

Now we are ready to create your marketing plan. To clarify, this is YOUR marketing plan for YOUR local operation. Perhaps your franchisor provides you with a marketing manual and a marketing calendar with key initiatives being rolled out by them throughout the quarter. That's great, but more is needed. We are suggesting you use that information in conjunction with your own marketing plan.

This is a very simple, yet, extremely powerful process. Do not expect a whole lot of bells and whistles with colorful charts and graphs, just brass tacks, nuts and bolts planning. We have spent some time going over your target marketing and positioning. I hope you did that.

Before we get started on your marketing plan, make sure you measure your position against the four criteria discussed previously. Just to review, 1) does it offer a benefit that your target audience really wants; 2) is it really a good, true to life benefit; 3) does it truly differentiate you from your competition; and 4) is it unique and difficult to copy.

Important: If you are not completely satisfied with these answers continue searching for a proper position because an accurate marketing position requires clear, constructive goals and effort. Positioning is a key to marketing. No guerrilla would ever consider doing any marketing at all without a proper marketing plan that includes a clear positioning statement.

Before writing your marketing plan, practice thinking big. This is your opportunity to stretch yourself. At this time, imagination should not be a limiting factor, so really open up your mind to all the possibilities for your future. Quite honestly, most marketing plans, especially when they are reduced to their simplest form, seem deceptively simple. A complete marketing plan, which can run as short as three paragraphs, includes: 1) the marketing plan, 2) the creative plan, and, 3) the media plan. Or, it can run as long as ten or even one hundred pages, which I definitely would not recommend, but anywhere from three paragraphs to as many pages as you would like, should serve as a guide.

Naturally, the marketing plan identifies the market and it provides the framework for creating advertising, it specifies the media to be utilized along with the costs. Rather simple, but truthfully, that is all it really needs to include. A business plan may require support documents, such as results of research, financial projections, the competitive situations, and other details. These details should not be included in the marketing plan itself.

Guerrilla marketing plans are brief, to the point, simple to understand, and easy to use. For example, a good roadmap will include the name or number of the highway wherever appropriate, but not every single road in the area. Include what is necessary, but nothing else. The marketing plan should be the essence of simplicity. The briefer your plan, the easier it will be to follow. You can bolster it with as many support documents as you wish, but do not include support information in the plan itself. Leave the details for the other documents.

One of the goals with the finished plan is that it be easy for your employees to immediately understand your goals and to see that your strategy is clear and direct. Many companies do not even let their employees see their marketing plans. This is a mistake. They need to be able to see it and understand it. Once you have given your plan the proper focus, you can expand it in those areas pertinent to your business. As you do so, remember, your main purpose is to obtain what? That's right…maximum profits. As we have discussed, profits are very different from sales. Anyone can achieve sales. It takes a guerrilla to consistently turn honest profits.

What will your finished plan look like? If you are one of those people who really likes colored graphs and charts you can put those in a nice binder with a great looking title page. Be proud of it. Your marketing plan is the heart of your business, but as far as the content, it should start out very brief. At first, you are going to try to state it clearly and effectively in one paragraph. Why do we call it the seven step marketing plan? Because we are going to come up with seven sentences. Your assignment after we finish this section will be to spend some time coming up with those seven sentences. I am first going to outline them, and then we will go into them in a little bit more detail.

Sentence #1

Purpose   Explain the purpose of your marketing. What is the overall goal of your marketing? What is it you are trying to accomplish? To drive trial or offer another soft step?

Sentence #2

How   Using your benefits list and your competitive advantages list, explain how you will achieve this purpose. Describe your competitive advantages and your benefits.

Sentence #3

Describe   Describe your target market or markets. You may have several target markets or just a specific one.

Sentence #4

Tools   Outline the marketing tools you will employ. With the more than 100 marketing weapons available, you will not be using all of them. Which ones apply best to your products and your business right now? You should use around ten weapons to begin.

Sentence #5

Niche   Describe your niche. What unique niche does your product fill?

Sentence #6

Identity   Reveal the identity of your company. What will customers and prospects think about your company when they see or hear about it? What does your business stand for?

Sentence #7

Budget   State your budget. This should be expressed as a percentage of your projected gross revenues. Keep in mind that most companies do not invest nearly enough money in their marketing. This is above and beyond your marketing royalty you pay to corporate.

Here are two examples of how this will look and sound. One example is a fictitious company and the other is real.

Pretend you own Betty's Bird Beds. You plan to sell bird cages to the end user, who currently owns a bird. Let your strategy start with something like this. The **purpose** of Betty's Bird Beds is to sell the maximum amount of bird cages at the lowest possible price. This will be **accomplished by** positioning the cages as being so valuable to the bird owner that they are guaranteed to be more valuable to the bird owner than the price they paid. The **target market** will be people who currently own a bird or birds. The **marketing tools** we plan to use include targeted direct mail campaigns, advertisements in newspapers and magazines, E-mailings to people that own birds, cross-promotions with pet stores, website and on-line store. The **niche** Betty's Bird Beds occupies is a business that provides high quality designer bird houses for people with birds. Our **identity** will be one of upscale creative bird houses for the bird lover. **Ten percent** (including what we pay to corporate) of our gross sales will be allocated to marketing.

The second example is for Computer Ace. The **purpose** of Computer Ace marketing is to fill 100 percent of the company's available time for computer education at the lowest possible cost per hour. This will be **done by** establishing the credentials of the educators, location of the operation, and the equipment. The **target market** will be local business people who can benefit from learning how to operate a small computer. The **marketing tools** that will be used include a combination of personal letters, circulars, brochures, signs on off-line and on-line bulletin boards, classified ads in local newspapers, Yellow Page advertising, direct mail, advertising specialties, free seminars, and publicity in local newspapers, on radio and on television. The company will be **positioned** (niche) as the prime source of one-on-one guaranteed instruction in the operation of small computers. Positioning will be intensified by an on-line presence in the local community, office décor, employee attire, telephone manners, selection and location. Our company's **identity** will be a blend of professionalism, personal attention, and warm human regard for students. **Ten percent** of sales will be allocated to marketing. Pretty simple and straightforward isn't it? We covered all seven things.

The plan starts with the purpose of the marketing. In other words, it starts with the bottom line in mind. Then it connects with the benefits that will beautify that bottom line and with those who will contribute to that line, the target audience. The marketing tools are then listed. Next is the positioning statement which explains what the product stands for, why the offering has value and why it should be purchased. The identity comes after that and we wrap it up with the investment, or budget.

With those three examples, you should be able to work on your marketing plan. **So, let's get to work. Use this space provided to create your seven sentence marketing plan.**

EXECUTE and TAKE ACTION

Marketing Plan For _____

_____

_____

_____

_____

_____

_____

_____

_____

_____

_____

_____

_____

YOUR CREATIVE STRATEGY

Your Designated Guerrilla – A Must!

Let's face it, the reality of running a franchise business is knowing exactly what you have to do and not having enough time to do it.

Here's the deal. Marketing can succeed only if time and energy are devoted to it regularly. And I really mean regularly and consistently. Insight and understanding, savvy and skill, are useless and wasted unless action is taken and somebody is paying close attention to the marketing process. Maybe that somebody will be you, but perhaps you are too busy attending to the details of the operations, the finance, productions, sales, or service. If that is the case, then you should hire somebody else to be your designated guerrilla, an individual who has the expertise, interest, desire, and the time to mastermind your marketing.

Select that person from within your company or from the outside. There are a lot of hired guns who would be delighted to eat, sleep, and obsess over your marketing. Just be sure you select somebody. In the businesses that I have owned over the years, I have been the designated guerrilla because I love marketing. Perhaps you can tell. To me it is a blast! But, perhaps you do not care too much for marketing, and your strengths lie in the operations or the financial aspects of the business. If so, you can delegate this one. That's fine. Just find someone who will approach the marketing function in true guerrilla fashion, with enthusiasm, confidence, high energy, and of course a killer instinct. If the person running your marketing show now does not have those attributes, you have got to get yourself another designated guerrilla.

Marketing, for all its sophistication, is really just like a little baby. It needs constant time and attention, and it thrives best when it is nurtured and guided. Unless you and your designated guerrilla provide this parenting, your company will begin to fade from your customers' and your prospects' minds. The companies that get into trouble are often those that establish marketing momentum and then, shortsited, they move onto other things. Those other things should always include more and better marketing, because marketing is a continuing connective process and not a series of disconnected events.

Your designated guerrilla should be a person who knows how many marketing weapons are available to you, how many you can create right there in your own office, which ones are free, what your competition is up to, and what kind of new technology can help you. Perhaps your designated guerrilla will be your marketing director or your director of sales. Or it might be a marketing consultant, or the account supervisor at an ad agency. As I mentioned before, it might just be you. Just be sure that it is someone who shares your vision and absolutely loves every aspect about marketing. If you do not have a good one, you are going to miss a lot of opportunities. You will constantly be in a position where your marketing must react rather than act, and the spirit of your company will never quite shine through.

How Much Time to Spend on Marketing

How much time should your designated guerrilla spend attending to these actions required by guerrilla marketing? Obviously, the most time and energy will be necessary at the outset, when the planning is done. Less time will be required during the launch phase, when your weapons are fired, and still less time after that. But remember, constant time must be devoted as you sustain the attack. That time will be devoted to three tasks: 1) maintaining the attack, 2) tracking your marketing efforts, and, 3) developing improved marketing. Focusing on marketing can be some of your time and money best spent.

Thinking back to some of the many reasons for business failures, the inability to market aggressively and constantly ranks right up there near the top. When that happens, the finger of fault always points to who? That's right, to you, the franchise owner, the person who is too busy with other business functions to give proper attention to marketing. Or, maybe you are too egotistical to delegate, I hope not; or, too ignorant of the power of marketing to realize the need for consistent nurturing. Do not fall into this trap. Get, and maintain a designated guerrilla.

Section Two

GUERRILLA PLANNING

100+ Marketing Weapons for Franchisees

WHEN IT COMES TO marketing weapons, tactics and strategies we could have written a book entitled, 1001 Ways to Market Your Business, or 400 ways, etc. The fact is, you don't need that many and as a busy franchisee you very likely don't have the time to plow your way through hundreds of marketing strategies.

We have narrowed the thousands of ways to market your business down to those that work...those that have been tried, proven, and tested over time. Are there other ideas out there? Absolutely! Guerrilla Marketing is about being creative. The goal here is to get your creative juices flowing. As you read through this next section, find the weapons that interest you, that you feel will work for you, and build upon them.

To help you navigate through the different weapons we have categorized them into the following categories:

- Local Store Marketing
- Non-Media Marketing
- Promotional Marketing
- Telephone Marketing

- Mini-Media Marketing

- Targeted Media Marketing

- Traditional Media Marketing

Your job, as a franchise owner, or designated guerrilla, is to do what you can to use as many weapons as possible. We've created a page available for download in the Franchise Training Center (www.franchisetrainingcenter.com) to help you categorize them into one of four categories. Login, go to the "Resource Center," and scroll down to the excel spreadsheet called "Choosing Your Marketing Weapons."

- List A will be the weapons you currently use and are using correctly.

- List B is the marketing weapons you use now but are not using them as effectively as possible.

- List C is the weapons that you are not using but you should be, and will begin using immediately.

- List D is the weapons that are not appropriate for your business at this time.

Keep these lists in front of you as you read, placing each marketing weapon in the appropriate category.

LOCAL STORE MARKETING

LET'S START by focusing within the four walls of your business. First of all, it is absolutely crucial that you DO NOT increase traffic into your store or location until you can create an excellent customer service experience. There are many books written that focus just on customer service alone. Of course I am a little partial to mine, Service...Some People Just Don't Get It! You can learn more about it during your one-month unlimited free access at The Franchise Training Center.

Whether my book or someone else's, and whatever it takes be sure you master customer service. No marketing can compensate for poor performance by employees once prospects or customers are in the store. No marketing campaign can succeed without killer execution on the customer service side. If you are not ready with the employees and the experience, HOLD ON! Don't do any more marketing until you nail that one.

Remember, to deliver killer customer service you must train for it. Not just once. Not just twice, but continually, at a minimum, monthly. Those companies that are truly successful have customer service training weekly. The meeting is sometimes as simple as "one minute meetings" with management teams. But they have them.

Internal Customer Marketing

Before we market to our external customers we need to market to our *internal customers*, our employees. If our employees aren't behind a marketing campaign it will flop. Hands down! We need to get our employees involved as much as possible in our marketing and marketing campaigns. Employees are our greatest asset. They are the front lines. The more excited they are about your marketing and marketing initiatives the more successful everyone will be, including you. Before thinking too much about marketing outside your location remember, your employees are your first priority.

Many books have been written about employee motivation. We will cover some essentials though you may wish to explore these principles in more detail.

☞ **Hire the right people.** When it comes to employees, mistake number one for most businesses is not taking enough time to get the "right" people. You can be sure if you can consistently hire the right employees, you have won half the battle. You should be recruiting constantly. Give employee referral incentives, and even customer referral incentives. Hold weekly open interviews. Get your key employees involved. Let them help in the process.

I know a franchise owner, Duane Costa with Cold Stone Creamery in California, who provides, hands down, some of the best customer service in the Cold Stone system. When asked how he does it he mentioned he gets his employees involved and holds "auditions." They only hire about 4 out of every one hundred applicants. They need to be actors, very into performing and very friendly. They make no exceptions. And they make great profits.

☞ **Employee of the month programs.** These programs are very under rated. In all the studies I've seen, money is not the most important part of employees' jobs. The most important thing is recognition for a job well done. It doesn't cost money to recognize and highlight star performers.

☞ **Team unity.** Team unity is built by spending fun times together outside of work. Successful franchise companies have company picnics, go bowling together, go boating, or even just meet occasionally at the movies. Assign someone on your team to be in charge of these activities or have a committee. Employees love this. Just like a tight athletic team, the better your employees know each other, understanding how individuals operate and what makes them tick, the better they perform on the field, so to speak.

☞ **Encourage employees to come up with promotional ideas themselves.** Perhaps you've noticed, as have I, that most people think "their idea" is the best. It's human nature to want our ideas implemented. Ideas that come from within the ranks of your own employees will often get much better "buy in." Why? Because it is "their" idea and they therefore take more ownership of it.

Also, before rolling out marketing ideas or campaigns, get feedback from employees on how it might best be rolled out. If you use an employee's idea you will be amazed at how they will get the entire staff charged up about it.

☞ **Constantly Share marketing results with your staff.** Use graphs or charts in the back room to help them get a visual understanding of how things are working. They will be able to see at a glance what is working and what is not. Again, information is power. The more you empower employees, the more buy in you get.

☞ **Marketing Training.** Make marketing a part of new employee training. Train employees from day one that they are the company's ambassadors and it is part of their job to help increase your sales and profits.

☞ **Friends and Family Discounts.** Give out family discount cards for employee's family and friends. After all, they are your customers too. Plus, this is a nice way to show your thanks and add more "perks" to the job.

☞ "Friends and Family Night. Building on the idea above, once per quarter have a night that friends and family can come in for a special discount. It's a great opportunity for you as the owner or manager to meet the family and see just why their kid turned out the way they did. No really, it's a good way to show the friends, family, and employees that you care. Everyone wants their employer to give more. This is a simple way to do it.

☞ Employee Discounts. Many franchise locations give employee discounts. Restaurants give food discounts. Clothing stores give discounts on clothing. Some companies offer a discount during the employee's shift. Seriously consider giving them the discount during "off the clock" times as well? Why? Because most people will bring friends in with them and they will spend money while they are there.

☞ Employees hand out flyers/coupons to neighbors, friends, at school etc. Make it a contest occasionally (if your employees hang out with your target market of course) to have employees hand out promotional vouchers or coupons and give awards for the most redeemed; a way for employees to earn extra cash while giving your business great exposure.

Again, there are tons of ways to motivate employees, and we have just touched on a few. Try some of these and your sales will increase, guaranteed.

☞ Database Marketing. This is, by far, one of the most effective things you will ever do. Build a customer database. If you are in a business that collects customer information as part of your business, it's a piece of cake; just be sure to market to them on a regular basis. If you are in a business that doesn't get customer's information, BEGIN IMMEDIATELY. These are customers that have come to you. Capture their information and market to them. How? Simple—just ask them to join your mailing list. Preferably collect their email address and let them know you will be sending them quarterly or monthly special offers. Let them know you will not be giving their information to anyone else. Be sure to honor that promise.

If it's a rainy day and you have a business that is slow on those days, send out an email with a coupon valid on that day only.

If you don't do this now because you don't have the time to enter the information or don't have the resources to manage it, we can steer you in the right direction. There are companies out there that do it all for you. Call 877-568-1212 for more information.

☞ **Mobile Marketing.** "80 million customers have used text messaging. In June 2005, cell phone customers sent 7.2 billion messages using the text feature built into most phones." —*Brand Republic 25 Oct 2005.*

"A survey found that 79% of businesses that used SMS said it was more effective than other marketing channels or loyalty tools." —*Brand Republic 25 Oct 2005*

Nuts and Bolts of Mobile Marketing

- Build a TEXT database to send incentives or periodic promotions. Imagine sending an instant coupon on a slow day to drive traffic.

- Build an EMAIL database to announce new products, and promotions.

- Track all advertising for effectiveness with TEXT. It promotes an immediate response. (print, radio, billboards, in-store etc.)

For more information on mobile marketing visit www.franchisemobilemarketing.com

☞ **Community Center.** Create a community board or even a community wall. Although franchise businesses are successful because they look like and are generally well known brands, people like to know they are locally owned and operated. This is one way to create that experience and deliver that message. Here are some things you can put on that board:

- Pictures of you and your family with the caption, "Locally owned and operated by the _____ family."

- Pictures of your team members with their names and their favorite movie, or their favorite song; something to personalize it so customers can connect.

- Past successful fundraiser information as well as new fundraisers coming up.

☞ **Customer Wall of Fame.** Take pictures of "regulars" and list the favorite item they purchase while patronizing your business. Have them sign their picture to make them feel even more important.

☞ **Trivia question of the day.** This is something team members can have a blast with. If you have a location near a movie theatre, they could be movie trivia questions. If it's during some sporting play-offs, the questions could be geared toward that. Whatever your trivia promotion is you may want to consider giving a discount to customers when they get it right. It is a great way to create a fun environment for your customers.

☞ **Always A Party.** I like to live by the theory that "commotion equals promotion." You've seen how people slow down to look closely when there is an accident on the freeway. It is human nature to look at a crowd and wonder, "What's going on?" The same thing happens when you create commotion around your store. Besides, just about everyone can use more fun in their day. Occasionally blow up balloons and put them outside on your front door, patio, and throughout your store. People may ask what's going on. Your answer is simple, you are celebrating the fact that they are there, or you are celebrating your great products, etc. Have some fun with it. You'll find this one also helps with visibility. People that generally may just pass by will stop and look.

☞ **Game On.** If you are in a high walk-by traffic location create a wheel (like on wheel of fortune but much smaller; perhaps out of a dart board.) Let people spin it for a prize. Make sure everyone gets at least a coupon to use in your store. You may also give out t-shirts, promotional mugs, and other accessories with your logos on them. Again, this follows the "commotion equals promotion" idea.

☞ **Become an art gallery.** The Wildflower Restaurant in Phoenix displays art from local schools for a week or so at a time. Why? The kids bring their parents in to see their "famous" picture proudly displayed on the wall of the restaurant. And yes, very likely, the family will eat while they are there as well. You know, one gets hungry looking at great artwork. This also shows people that you are involved in the community and giving back whenever possible.

☞ **Give out promotional items.** Jack in The Box even sells them. Maybe you've seen the "Jack" for the antenna of your car. You can sell promotional items for a nominal amount or simply give them away. The only rule here is to make sure it has your logo on it. Key chains, lanyards, Frisbees, blow up beach balls, mini footballs, antenna balls, etc.

☞ **Offer free popcorn/drinks/ice cream etc.** if you are NOT a food establishment. Especially if people need to wait in a line or wait for a cell phone to get fixed if you own an electronics store, it can be very classy to offer waiting customers a soft drink etc.

☞ **Good neighbor marketing.** Start with businesses around your location. If you have a location within a retail center create a "good neighbor" discount card and give to all the businesses to give to their employees to use in your business. This is a captive audience. They are there nearly every day of the week. Get them as customers. As you provide excellent service for them they will talk about you and actually send people your way.

The best example was with our Jamba Juice stores. We gave a "good neighbor" discount to Office Max a few doors down. When they had a "customer appreciation day" they asked us if we wanted to come down and give out free samples to hundreds of their customers. And we said a resounding "YES." Do you see how a small thing like a "good neighbor discount" can snowball into some great things?

☞ **Free day or discount day for employees.** If you are near businesses pick one a week and invite them in (generally through the human resource department) for a freebie or a great deal. Get them hooked on your product. Whether the invited business comes over on that particular day or not you have exposure in their store.

☞ **Business to business.** This can be a blast! Get a team of two people together to go building to building and hand out free promotional items. If you deliver or if you accept fax orders let them know. If you own a smoothie business dress up like a banana and have some fun with it. If you own a cell phone store, dress up like a big cell phone. People will remember it. If they haven't had your product before, give them an aggressive discount. If they are a regular customer, perhaps you have a different coupon that isn't quite as aggressive.

This is an ongoing process. Get a map (even a hand drawn one) of the businesses you hit and the date you do it. Start close to your store and work your way out up to a mile or two. It works. In fact, it is far more effective than any print advertising you will ever do!

☞ **Sample within and outside your business.** It's no secret that when you have a great product and you get people to taste it or to use it, they will very often become a customer. Not only will they become a customer, but you may also be creating some buzz. The key to product trial is that you must have a quality product otherwise it will backfire. For that reason, the sample itself must be outstanding.

Logo Mania. Everywhere you go wear your company shirt. It's amazing how effective this is. I see many franchise owners that perhaps are tired of wearing the company uniform, so they don't. Wear it proudly. It will strike up conversations and give you the opportunity to talk about your business. Wrap your car or at least get your company logo on it. Build your brand wherever you go.

NON-MEDIA MARKETING WEAPONS

NON-MEDIA MARKETING WEAPONS, in many instances, don't cost money to implement. These are the marketing weapons you may not generally think of as marketing, but they are, and they are powerful.

As you go through this section, keep in mind we know that some of the marketing weapons such as *your company name*, *your theme line* or *logo* are already set for you by your franchisor. However, hundreds if not thousands of new franchise companies are created each year, and many who are in the creating phase of business may be reading this book.

As a franchisee, how do you represent and fully leverage the name, logo, and theme line of your company?

Your Marketing Plan: As we discussed earlier, most people, when it comes to marketing plans, fall into one of a few categories. Ranging from having a big and complicated plan to not having one at all. For others who have a marketing plan, the use of it could fall somewhere along the scale of only using it occasionally. The last are those who have an effective, useful, brief plan and use it regularly. If you are not in the last category, we'll help you get there. This one weapon alone will launch you far ahead of your competition. Hopefully, you have completed your own seven step marketing plan and you are beginning to use it.

☞ **Your Marketing Calendar:** The marketing calendar is in the same category as the marketing plan because they go hand in hand. Understand this very important concept about your marketing calendar, it is part of your marketing blueprint. It is your map. Successful franchisees have one and use it regularly. We recommend having at least 6 months planned out. Projecting the next 12 to 18 months is even better. Have you done this before? Have you ever been so organized and disciplined in your marketing? I hope so. But if not, the concepts in this book will help. Your marketing calendar is a crucial weapon for your success. If you would like a spreadsheet to help you with this, visit the Franchise Training Center under "resources."

☞ **Your Market Niche:** Market niche is also known as positioning. This has reference to what you will stand for in the minds of your prospects and customers. Several years ago there was an airline that established such a solid marketing plan it took off with astounding speed. It positioned itself as a high frequency no frills airline that specialized in flights of less than two hours and in connecting passengers with long distant routes of other airlines. It was a unique position because no one else at the time offered this service on the level they did. Success came rather easily.

Interestingly enough, during the airline challenges of a few years ago, this airline was one of the few that remained profitable despite the major downturn in airline travel. Other airlines over the years have followed this positioning and tried to offer the same service but don't do it quite as effectively. Who is it? Southwest Airlines. So what niche do you and your company fill? This is a great way to set yourself apart from the competition with your own marketing niche.

☞ **Your Company Name:** Believe it or not, the name of your company is a marketing weapon. There are good names and there are bad names. I remember the commercial a few years ago that used several funny examples of the use of company names. One segment was a teenage boy applying for a job as if he was in an interview. He was telling the audience that he was a great babysitter, very reliable, and that he loved kids. He was applying for the job of being your babysitter. Everything he said was comforting, he looked great, looked reliable. I was almost ready to hire him myself to watch my own five kids. Then at the end of the segment it gave his name and phone number. Guess what it was? Freddy Kruger. The trailer on the commercial said something like this, "Use a name you can trust." The sad part is, I can remember the commercial, but not the product.

Branding your franchise company name takes time. If you are involved in a large franchise company this won't be so tough. If your franchise isn't very well established yet, use every opportunity to get the name of your company out there.

Your Identity: An identity conveys your company's personality throughout your entire marketing. Make sure your marketing realistically reflects who you are and what you stand for. To me, there is nothing worse than patronizing a business after seeing one of their ads (or nine of their ads because it usually takes nine exposures to an ad to get people to take action), and being let down because they really are not who they say they are. Has this ever happened to you? I am sure it has.

Too often, companies create a false image by conveying themselves as being much better than they really are.

Remember, do not create a false sense of who you are and what your company will deliver. As a franchisee it is so important that you deliver on what your commercials say you will.

Your Logo: Some people call the logo their trademark symbol. Whichever term you prefer, logo or trademark, it is a graphic image and it is more a visual than verbal representation of your company. Think of how important the "swoosh" has been to Nike over the years. What about how fast the company Target has made an impression with the red and white target they use in all of their marketing? Good logos can be very powerful. Use yours whenever and wherever possible.

☞ **Your Theme Line:** A theme line is a set of words that summarizes your company or its prime benefits. The longer you use the theme, the better, so choose a theme line you can live with for a long time. For example, how long have people been in the, "Good hands of All-state?" How long has Rice Krispies, "Snapped, crackled and popped?" How long has the Jolly Green Giant been around? How long has Campbell's soup been "Mmm, Mmmm, good?" Some companies change their themes way too often. Get a theme and stick with it and it can be a very, very powerful marketing weapon.

☞ **Your Meme:** It is a safe bet that most people do not know what a meme is. Here is a story to help describe it. A meme is something that has actually been around forever but only recently has been used more and more in advertising.

In Guerrilla Marketing, a meme's purpose is to instantly profit, sell, motivate, and communicating how your product preserves and improves lives.

For example, a meme can be words like "Lean Cuisine," pictures like the Marlboro Cowboy, or sounds from the Valley of the Jolly Green Giant. How about actions? The Clydesdales pulling the Budweiser wagon, or imagery, like Burger King's flame broiled hamburgers.

For Guerrillas, a meme is a concept that has been so simplified anybody can understand it instantly and easily. Within two seconds you must convey who you are and why someone should buy from you instead of a competitor and trigger an emotional response that generates a desire.

☞ **Your Hours of Operation:** Here is a marketing weapon that has differentiated many companies recently. It is critical that you make it easy for people to do business with you and your company. Customers want you to be there when they are available. They do not care about your inconvenience. We live in a 24/7/365 era. To effectively use this weapon you need to be available for your customers.

One example is a fishing store that opens at 5:00 a.m. to catch the fisherman on his way to the river or lake who stops for last minute supplies. It would be especially impressive to offer coffee, juice, and donuts to create an even bigger impact.

Certainly you've seen the push in fast food to be open until 2:00 a.m. in the morning. Some are even open 24 hours. Because of the opportunity to buy things online, all day and all night long, people have come to expect this same convenience in other purchases. The internet never sleeps. Because of this new expectation you need to make sure you use your hours of operation as an effective marketing weapon.

☞ **Your Days of Operation:** Closely related to your hours of operation are your days of operation. Just like your hours of operation, the days of the week you are open matters just as much. Dentists and others in various medical fields are staying open late one or two nights a week and including half a day on Saturday to increase their business.

Take a close look at your days of operation. Are you accessible enough? If not, you may want to consider a change. I remember many years ago we chose to keep our Jamba Juice stores closed on Sundays. One year later we chose to be open seven days a week, more out of necessity than anything else. Sundays became one of our most profitable days in several locations. Our downtown location, since it was mostly business people who worked Monday through Friday, never did well on Sundays. It was important for us to be flexible with different locations to meet the needs of the customer.

The days of the week you are open depends on the particular business you are in and on your location. Be sure to examine it carefully and if your competition is open, you'd better be open too. Remember, you need to use your days of operation as one of your marketing weapons.

☞ **Your Neatness:** Here is an idea that most people would not classify as a marketing strategy, but it is. Neatness! And it is powerful! Perhaps people ignore it because it is so simple and easy. The fact is, messiness turns off many a customer. In the customer's mind it is generally believed that the messiness carries over into all aspects of the business.

How many times have you heard someone say, "I go there just because they have clean restrooms"? Just a few months ago when interviewing a customer, I found out that he bypasses several gas stations either on the way to or the way from work to go to the Chevron station because they have nice restrooms. Nice and clean. I was shocked I would expect customers to have that kind of cleanliness expectation for restaurant bathrooms, but not a gas station.

Many underestimate the importance of cleanliness to customers and prospects. This should be a wakeup call to all! Neatness carries over to your building, your lobby, your floors, your employee attire, your company vehicles. Any contact your customer has with you or your company should always be neat.

☞ **Your Strategic Alliances:** As you begin to establish yourself in a competitive market niche with a well-thought-out marketing strategy, you're in a position to build strategic alliances. There is no question about the importance of this weapon because all successful marketing is based upon relationships. Sometimes they are short-lived, non-emotional, and fairly shallow relationships, but each sales transaction or social interaction of any kind is an opportunity for the guerrilla to improve each relationship.

Remember, from a business perspective, a relationship is far more important than just making a sale. Relationships lead to referral sales, repeat sales, volume sales, and dependable sales. The deeper your relationships with your customer, the greater profits you will earn. Great guerrilla relationships come from six primary groups: customers, employees, suppliers, the media, businesses in your community, and anyone else with whom you can reap the benefits of a mutually beneficial relationship.

Customer service is its own marketing weapon and covered in detail on its own. We will focus next on relationships. First, Guerrillas should use a sharing mentality whenever possible. The "I'll scratch your back if you scratch mine" mentality is an excellent business and life practice for that matter. All successful marketers get more out of the marketing process when they work with others instead of against others, unless of course they are your direct competitor, in which case you need to very politely out-maneuver them.

Consistent success and growth will belong to teams, not players. Teams possess a strength and durability not dreamed of by the lone wolf entrepreneur. The solution to long-term success is relationships called strategic alliances. Businesses that flourish will not be companies that are independent firms characterized by the one-man-band entrepreneur. Instead, they will be dependent firms that need one another to prosper as small or even gigantic businesses. These companies will depend on each other for expertise, money, service and the way they are perceived by customers. The dependence will be a strategic alliance. The strategy is to increase profits.

Unlike standard partnerships and other joint ventures, strategic alliances will be as much for the short term as for the long term.

With whom will you form these alliances? There are more opportunities than you think. Suppliers, competitors from your own area, competitors from distant areas, businesses with the same audience, businesses in your community, private investors, your employees, your bank, your landlord, your service providers, just to name a few.

The key to establishing and maintaining strategic alliances is cooperation. You must think in terms of cooperation rather than competition. Here is the goal: a network of contacts and colleagues each increasing their individual profits by helping you increase yours. Strategic alliances combine the essential ingredients of a successful business including: planning, marketing, technology, inventory, people and money.

The ultimate aim of the alliance is the success of the alliance. With that big goal and that big list of ingredients, it may take several allies to form a real slam-dunk strategic alliance. If it is successful, the small businesses within it will be successful. Believe me, with the proper allies, small business success rates will soar.

Think partnerships. Think about how you can help others in your strategic alliance. Members of a strategic alliance get together for meetings monthly, quarterly, or semi-annually. It really depends on the group and its needs. If it makes sense geographically then be sure to get together in person for meetings. If not, at least have meetings on the phone. On a real practical level, I know many business alliance groups who get together to share leads.

If you aren't invited to be in an alliance, create your own. Most guerrillas need to take the bull by the horns and get it going themselves. Use strategic alliances to your advantage. Begin by making a list of people you think you can form an alliance with and get after it.

☞ **Your Fusion Marketing Partners:** Building strategic alliances will create opportunities for fusion marketing. This type of marketing embodies the very spirit of a strategic alliance. By combining marketing efforts, alliances are able to increase their marketing exposure while decreasing their marketing costs. Fusion marketing differs from strategic alliances in that strategic alliances focus on helping each other but fusion marketing takes it a step further and entails joint marketing together.

Find a complementary company with yours and market together. I am sure you have seen fusion marketing in action, you'll be watching a commercial and think it's for Coca Cola and then, ten seconds into the commercial, up pops McDonald's. In your mind you think, "Oh, this is a McDonald's commercial," when all of a sudden out swims Nemo, the orange black and white clown fish, advertising his big début in the movie, "Finding Nemo." Many large companies do this all the time but it is not limited to large companies when you work with strategic alliances. Businesses of all sizes can benefit from fusion marketing.

It can be almost any combination if it makes sense and believe it or not in some situations fusion marketing partners don't seem to mix at all but it can still be effective. Some common fusion partners may be a doctor and a dentist, a doctor and a chiropractor. That is why you see medical plazas together all the time. They feed off each other: a car wash with a car dealer, a video store with an ice cream store, a hair salon with a woman's clothing store, a smoothie company and a health food market. You get the idea. Find your fusion marketing partners and get to work.

☛ **Your Guarantee and/or Your Warranty:** Here is another marketing weapon that most would not consider marketing. I'm confident you would agree that it is tough these days to find a good guarantee or warranty. Everywhere I turn I am asked if I want to buy an extended warranty. The other day I was in buying some carrots and I was asked by the produce clerk if I wanted to buy an extended warranty. I'm kidding of course, but seriously, what happened to the good old days when things were backed by the seller?

When I have purchased televisions, computers, or other high-ticket items I always get asked if I want to purchase an additional warranty. I think it's very odd that they ask this question just after I've been told that my purchase is really the top of the line, absolutely awesome, and won't break down. How ironic is that? Why do I need a warranty protecting it from breaking over the next 12 months if it's as good as they say it is? Shouldn't it last longer than that anyway?

You should back your product in the best way possible. People do not like risk. That is why so many good companies offer risk free 30 day trials. This is a great sales strategy. Why do you think they use it in a pet store? You know why! The kids bring you in, they fall in love with a puppy, they give you their own puppy dog face (you know the one I am talking about) and then they say, "Please, please, please, can we buy him, Daddy, please?" At that point the pet store salesman says to you, "You know, why don't you take him home for the night, just for a test drive?" If you do, you are in trouble, because usually you will also fall in love with the dog. You can use this approach with many, but of course not all, products and services.

My wife and I were at dinner at Auggie's. We go there often. They have great steaks. I love the steaks, but this time my wife's steak came out cooked completely wrong. The great server not only redid it for her but gave us a $25.00 voucher off of our next visit. That was going above and beyond on a warranty. The server definitely "WOWED" us and we went there again the following week.

Warranties and guarantees are powerful because they demonstrate company integrity. And for those of you who do sell extended warranties, please do not take offense. I understand that is a great way to offer commission for your salespeople, but please back up your product or service. It is so important to take care of the customer because one upset customer will tell 15 to 20 people about that one bad experience. It is much less expensive to take care of your customer, to make them happy and turn them into a good word of mouth machine. By the way, make sure you ask them for referrals right after you take care of them.

☛ **Your Follow-Up Plan:** Sometimes business owners get so busy attracting new business they fail to employ this all-important marketing weapon. One of the primary differences between a Guerrilla and a non-Guerrilla is that non-Guerrillas think the marketing is over once they make the sale, but the Guerrilla knows the real marketing begins after the sale has been completed. The idea is to have long term relationships with that customer and the people that customer knows. And the raw truth is, that will not happen if you quit marketing once you have made the sale.

Most business lost these days is not due to poor quality or high prices or poor service. Most business is lost because customers are totally ignored after the sale. This example will explain. Suppose you earn $100.00 profit every time you make a sale. If you are a Guerrilla, within 48 hours you send the customer a thank you note expressing gratitude for their business. When is the last time you received a thank you note from a business within 48 hours? Very few companies do this. That is why it is so powerful and that is why your customer will remember you and your company.

Within 30 days you send another note asking the customer if they have any questions or needs with what they purchased. Notice that you are not trying to make a sale here. Your customer will notice that too and as a result you will be on your way to making a friend which is a lot better than a customer. Within 90 days you send the customer a piece of mail or make a phone call informing him of a product or service available at a discount, preferably something related to his past purchase. Naturally you will add the customer to your newsletter list.

Then, six months later, you may send out a questionnaire to that same customer so you can find out as much information as possible about those who frequent your business. This information will be used in your future direct mail target marketing to help you reach out to those with similar interests as your current customers. Nine months from the sale you may send them something from one of your fusion marketing partners. Within ten months the customer receives a letter in a self addressed envelope requesting names and addresses of their friends who might enjoy being added to your mailing list.

Whether regular mail or email and within a year the customer gets an anniversary card commemorating the one year anniversary of them being your customer. How many companies do this? Not many. That is why it is so powerful. As a result of this warm inexpensive follow up, instead of making one purchase from you during the year, the customer makes three purchases. In addition to giving you the names of potential customers that you requested, your customer refers your business to at least four people during the course of a year, and instead of a one time transaction, your relationship with the customer and the referral customers lasts around 20 years. That one customer is worth about $400,000.00 in profits to you if you understand the power and the principle of follow up. That same person is worth only $100.00 in profits to you if you do not. That is a $399,900.00 difference.

☞ **Your Service and Your Employees:** The service you and your employees provide will always be a reflection of your leadership and the caliber of the employees you hire. How is it that a business becomes customer oriented? It begins with a desire to be that way and the energy to ensure that the desire spreads throughout your organization and remains there permanently. It all starts with you! You have to walk the talk first! Lead by example.

You will have those days that customers really get on your nerves and get you down, but hang on. You must represent what your company stands for at all times. Not just in front of your customers and prospects, but especially in front of your employees. Very often I have seen an owner or manager dealing with a bad customer situation and after the customer leaves they talk badly about them with the employee. What kind of message does this send?

If you have a challenge with this, please overcome it. Why? because you and your employees are such an important marketing weapon. To really master this weapon, you must practice one of the golden rules of successful guerrillas: "Always try to think like your customer. Walk a couple of miles in your customer's shoes. Look closely at your business through their eyes." Check out a business similar to yours. Honestly assess its methods of greeting you, its service, its identity, etc. What catches your attention? Determine what appeals to you. Focus on what would sell you.

When you instill customer service in your employees on a regular basis, you will see magic happen right before your eyes. To do this you must train consistently, even if you are tired of talking about it and think your employees are tired of hearing it. You must press on and pound this principle into the mind of everyone in your company. If you allow creativity in your employees, which I highly encourage, you will be amazed at some of the things you will see.

I want to share with you one of my favorite customer service stories ever. It is quite hilarious, but also drives the point home. One day, the Day-Timers,Inc. received a binder returned by a really unhappy customer. It seems her dog chewed her luxurious calfskin binder to shreds. It was not the company's fault, but what do you think the company did? That's right! They replaced the binder.

Now the best rule to follow when fixing a problem is this: do not just fix the problem, fix it with a perk. Well, that's what Day-Timers, Inc. did! Not only did they send a new binder, they also sent the customer a dog biscuit. Two weeks later, a thank you note appeared...from the dog. All of that information went into the computer and one year later, when it was time to send out the new Day Timer® calendars, the company sent this customer a second dog biscuit. Sure enough, a thank you note appeared from the dog. This time, there was a P.S. at the bottom of the card. It said "Got a problem. Cat is jealous." So the company sent over a can of cat food.

A third letter appeared, this one written by the owner of the animals, thanking Day-Timer, Inc. for its excellent customer service. However, there was a P.S. on the bottom of this thank you card that said "By the way, the dog really did not write the letters. The cat did." Do you think this customer will ever buy another brand other than Day-Timer®? Never! And this is really a true story. Believe me when I say this: How you treat your customers and prospects can be a very effective guerrilla marketing weapon.

☞ **Your Benefits**: Guerrilla marketers know that a major question on the mind of all prospects and customers is, "If I do business with this company what's in it for me?" That is why you need to continuously teach and train your employees on the benefits of your offering. As part of your seven step marketing plan you should have made a lengthy powerful benefits list. I suggested you have a meeting, or several, with your employees and at least one customer to come up with this list. Your customers may be doing business with you for many other reasons than the obvious ones so make sure you know all the benefits.

The wife of Jay Levison, the creator of Guerrilla Marketing, used to patronize a book store five miles away from their home rather than the one that was only one mile away. When he asked her why, she excitedly responded, "Their carrot cake." You can be sure the book seller had a benefits list focused on their selection, their personnel, their extended hours, their excellent lighting, their willingness to take phone orders, and their willingness to make deliveries, but unless they invited the customer to their benefits list meeting they probably would not realize the appeal of the carrot cake served in the café.

Make sure you identify every single benefit of your offering and then capitalize on it by telling the world.

Your Use of Technology and Computers: We live in an unbelievable time, the technology age. This can be a potent marketing weapon. I am sure you would agree that technology has been revolutionizing small business, enabling many small business owners to dream new dreams and attain them in surprisingly brief time spans. Sure, technology assists all businesses, but it assists small businesses in the greatest ways.

Technology gives small businesses a blatantly unfair advantage because it allows them to look big and act big without having to spend big. The price of credibility has plummeted while the achievement of credibility has become more precious. Technology provides small business owners with the ticket to credibility, in fact, a lifetime ticket. Until now, the advantages that small businesses could boast over big businesses were more personalized service, extra flexibility and speed.

Today guerrilla business owners have a secret weapon, technology. Technology is easier than ever, so easy that high tech is becoming easy tech. Technology has leveled the playing field. With a presence online, the practitioner of free enterprise can connect up with allies and customers anywhere in the community and on the entire planet. Virtual businesses are all over the place.

Many companies that are perceived as very large, nearly owning an entire industry, are being run out of a basement somewhere in northeast Idaho, because of the power of technology. No one knows the difference between the large and the small businesses. This creates a huge opportunity for all those who enter the world of free enterprise.

One of the greatest benefits of computers is the ability to produce top quality marketing pieces yourself at a fraction of the cost. Actually, there are many guerrilla marketing weapons that you can produce yourself on your computer: websites, newsletters, flyers, post cards, brochures, catalogs, gift certificates, coupons, signs, and computer design proposals, just to mention a few. All of these things are fairly easy to design with the software available today.

Technology helps the small business gain credibility and economy while providing speed and power. That is important in an age where credibility is crucial, economy is a necessity, speed is revered, and power comes from being part of a team. Credibility is earned by creating professional looking marketing materials which is economical to do on your own computer. It really can save you a lot of money.

Speed comes with cellular, wireless, pager, fax, email and voice mail technology. Power is gained from networking and sharing technology. Embrace technology. Use it to your advantage. If you are hesitant to use it because you do not understand it, get help! There are all kinds of help on this topic in the form of classes, books, and online courses. There is no reason not to be utilizing this powerful marketing weapon.

☞ **Your Selection:** It is a competitive marketplace. Prospects have many businesses to choose from. Your selection can really differentiate you from the competition. With so many choices available today, people have become accustomed to selection. With the benefit of free enterprise, having and providing many selections for the customer has become a necessity. People are looking for a business that offers a wide selection. They do not just want to pick from one or two colors, styles, and price ranges. They want a whole lot of choices. The more choices, the better, because they will take their money to a business that offers a broad selection

Look carefully at your selection. Are you using all the products your franchisor provides? Are you offering at least as much as your competition? And, more importantly, are you offering what your customers really want? Selection can be a very powerful guerrilla marketing tool. A good selection keeps customers coming back.

Your Contact with the Customer: Your contact time with your customer is very important. You must always remember that every moment you spend with a customer is a marketing opportunity. Use it to intensify your relationship, market other items, and be of better service. One of the most important human needs is for an identity. Make sure that you recognize the identity of your prospects and customers. Do not treat people as prospects. Do not treat them as members of a demographic group. Recognize their uniqueness and treat them as special individuals. The only way to do this is by spending time with them. This goes along with the fact that people buy from companies and people that they trust. Trust comes with time and consistency.

Even if you are in a business where you do not have one-on-one contact with customers and prospects, you can accomplish this with newsletters and other forms of contact. Just remember this, the more time you spend with prospects and customers, the more time you have to market to them.

Your "Giver" vs. "Taker" Mentality: I'm really hoping by now you see the power of giving, giving free information, free samples, free anything you can that will enhance the relationship between you and the customer. It is definitely the way to become an expert marketer. Some companies only take. Trust me on this: customers eventually see the difference and will always gravitate to the giving company. Just ask yourself, as a customer, would you be more attracted to a giver company or a taker company. The answer is obvious!

As your company's marketing honcho or designated guerrilla, would you describe your company as a giver or a taker? Be honest about this. Maybe this will help you think more clearly about this concept. Let's say you hear about an apartment building with 100 percent occupancy. That is not too unusual until you learn that the building is in an area where similar apartment buildings have only a 70 percent occupancy. When you dig a little deeper, you learn that the fully occupied building offers free auto grooming with each rental unit. Free auto grooming – what is that? It is a guerrilla marketing weapon that pays enormous dividends. It is also a service greatly appreciated by the tenants. Someone is hired to wash the tenants' cars weekly. Regardless of what you pay the person, it is insignificant compared with what 30 vacancies would cost.

It boils down to this: some companies are *giver* companies that relish giving things away to entice prospects and breed customer loyalty. Other companies are *taker* companies that offer nothing for which they do not charge. Make sure you and your company fall on the giving side of the fence. It will definitely make a big difference in your business.

☛ **Your Pricing:** If you develop a giver mentality, you are going to price competitively. Let's talk about pricing for a few moments. Whenever business slows, the temptation is to lower your prices. When people do not buy, the reason they give is often that the price is too high. Your friends and associates and employees will all tell you that you must lower your price. This does not make sense and there are a lot of reasons why.

First, extensive market research has shown that people often do not care that much about price. For instance, when ranking why they switched dry cleaners, customers gave the following reasons which are ranked by the importance they attached to each: 1) service, 2) location, 3) quality of workmanship and, 4) price. Notice, the number one reason was service or lack thereof, second was location, next was the quality of workmanship, (or lack of quality workmanship) and lastly was price. The same has been proven in banking, food, even automobile sales. Take a look at the best selling brands in any industry, from cigarettes to cars to jeans, and you will see that the lowest priced item is rarely the best selling item.

When a customer tells you your price is too high, what he is really saying is that you do not give enough value for what you are charging. Time and time again, aggressive businesses have shown that people will pay for quality and service.

There is an old saying that goes something like this, "There is always someone willing to make something a little shoddier and a little cheaper to charge a penny less."

As you consider your position in the market, realize that you can always out-deliver your competitors in service and convenience. And there is always someone out there who can beat you on price. You need to find your niche and defend it. Put another way, if all you have to compete with is price, how can you make a living? If your competitor is always willing to beat you by a dollar, the two of you will eventually find yourselves bankrupt.

Your goal shouldn't necessarily be to sell something cheaper than everyone else. Your goal is to deliver more value than your competitors. Value is created by understanding your customer's needs, not by selling your product for less money than anyone else. Focus on your customer's needs.

Focusing on customer's needs brings us to an important discussion: value pricing versus cost-based pricing. Many guerrillas are hung up on the idea that the price of an item has to have something to do with how much it costs to make. I am frequently asked for advice from businesses that have been determining their pricing by figuring out their out of pocket costs and adjusting upward. This method is guaranteed not to work. Here is why:

The customer could not care less what it costs you to make something. A person starving in the desert will gladly pay $1 million for a glass of water that costs you nothing. A screaming teenager will pay $40.00 to see a concert. The marginal profit on the ticket is $38.00.

Consumers are faced with this decision every time they contemplate buying something, "Is the money I will need to give up for this item worth less to me than the item itself?" Again, as long as the value of your product is greater than its price you will be able to sell it. Next time you price an item, do the pricing without figuring in how much it costs you to manufacture. Try to determine what a customer would be willing to pay—both with and without advertising—and then look at the cost. Do it backwards.

Guerrillas understand that offering consumers a good deal, consistently giving them more than they pay for, is the way to build customer loyalty.

☞ **Your Location, Your Location, Your Location:** Yes, you've heard it a thousand times before…location, location, location, location. I'd heard it too but I didn't understand it as well as I should have when I opened one of my first business locations. If you are in a terrible location right now and have done everything possible to drive business in and still are not as successful as you would like, seriously consider moving your business to a better location. Yes, it will cost money but you need to analyze everything to see if you will come out ahead in the long run. I did when I moved my business.

If you are looking for a new location, let me pass along this critical word of advice on what to look for. These tips are ideal for retail locations. It also stands to reason that if your customers don't come to your location to do business, then your ideal location is the location with the best rent you can find.

Nuts and Bolts of Choosing a Location

1. When choosing a location, **visibility** is the most important element. It does make a difference if you are on a pad out on the street or at least on an end cap. It is definitely worth the extra money it will cost you for visibility. You have to live with your location a long time so get it right the first time.

2. Another consideration is your **co-tenancy**. What other businesses are in the center? Are they the same quality as yours? Are they the businesses that share the same demographic as you do? Are they businesses that you can form alliances with?

3. Think about **accessibility**. Is there ample parking? What about during your busiest times? Is there enough parking then? Is your parking lot easy to get in and out of?

4. What about **the neighborhood or part of town that you are located in**? Are they your target market?

5. **Signage.** Can you get on the monument sign along the street? Remember, when it comes to signs bigger is better.

6. Remember this is your business and your space. You will be paying rent. **Don't let anyone talk you into it a location unless it has all the winning factors.**

☞ **Your Sales Training:** What a tragedy when customers come to you because of your great location but find that your people are not adequately trained. If you have sales people that work for you, how often do you hold training meetings? I hope you will respond with weekly or at least monthly. If you are in direct sales this is your most valuable weapon. Just like effective marketing requires repetition, sales training requires the same attention. The better equipped your sales people are at representing your product or service the higher the closing ratio will be. Do not skimp on sales training. Successful franchisees provide continual sales training.

Studies have proven this next concept time and time again: sales forces that are continually trained, produce higher results. Think about it this way, have you ever been to a seminar or workshop or a sales training class or meeting yourself? Of course you have. Wouldn't you agree that the first week after that meeting you tried extra hard to implement what you learned? What about the week after that. You probably made a great effort but by week three and week four, if you're like most folks, your excitement for the new approach began to fade. It is the same way with your sales force. Every few weeks when the sizzle begins to wear off and your sales people begin to drop back into their complacent routine, pump it up with more training.

The material doesn't have to be new and innovative every single meeting. Repetition is powerful. Role playing is excellent. What ever type of training you choose, just do it regularly and you will reap the rewards.

☞ **Your Quality:** A well-trained sales force understands what quality is. To be successful, at least if you plan on being around for a long time, please clearly understand that you've got to offer quality in your product or service. The guerrilla marketing attack is no shuck and jive show where you can just wing it. You've got to be devoted to excellence in your offering if marketing is going to work for you at all. If you offer excellence, the guerrilla marketing attack will motivate more people faster than standard marketing to buy what you are selling. If you don't offer quality, it will speed up your downfall and your demise. If you are selling substandard products, trust me, the word will get around.

Here's the problem with not offering quality. For every complaint you hear there are 26 other complaints you won't hear. Those 26 additional dissatisfied customers will tell an average of 15 to 20 other people about the problem they had with your business. Do not start your guerrilla marketing attack unless your offerings are excellent in quality and superb in value. Once they are, those offerings, plus a strong marketing attack, will make a potent combination.

☞ **Your Upgrade:** If you have an organization that is focused on quality, you will have greater opportunities to upgrade your customer. This is pretty straightforward and simple. McDonald's pioneered this one years ago with the Super Size campaign.

Once someone has ordered a product or service they are obviously interested in it and they like it so sell them more of it. Warranties and guarantees, which we covered earlier, are examples of upgrades. If you have a service, offer bronze, silver, and gold levels of service. I get this at carwashes all the time. If I order the basic wash they ask if I would like the VIP for just a few dollars more. If I order the VIP they ask me if I would like a hand wax for just a few dollars more. If I am at Banana Republic buying pants, they ask if I would like a shirt and some socks to go with it. If I go to McDonald's I get asked if I would like fries with that, or if I would like to Super Size my meal. Make no mistake about it, that extra 30 cents or extra few bucks really does add up.

To make the upgrade effective you need to train your salespeople to religiously ask people for the upgrade. Incentivize them for up-selling and adding on to their sales. If you do not use this weapon you are leaving way too much money on the table. Put some thought into this. What can you sell as an upgrade if you do not already? What can you add on to your sales that you currently are not? Believe me, if you put the effort behind this one, it will really pay off.

☞ **Your Research:** Research will help you in everything you do. A Guerrilla is always engaged in research. They research the market, the product, their service, their media options, their competition, their industry, their prospects, their customers, technology that can help them, their benefits, the internet and potential fusion marketing partners on and off line.

In marketing, knowledge is power. Understand your industry, the changes and the upcoming advances. Always stay ahead of your competition with knowledge and research. Research can be a roadmap to where you want to go in the future. It will pay great dividends.

☞ **Your Past Success Stories:** Most people do not like to be pioneers or guinea pigs when it comes to handing over their hard-earned money. Generally, most people like to hear about others that have gone before them, those who took the risk and experienced success with your product or services. That is why testimonials are so powerful. That is why we recommend reprinting and distributing the good articles about your company.

Your job is to convince prospects of your acceptance by the entire community or industry. Let each new customer know that he or she is not pioneering with you. Print your success stories in brochures, on your website, and in direct mail letters. Put a copy up in your lobby if you have one. The more specific you can be in sharing your customers' success stories the better. Just make sure you have permission from the customer or client before you use their story. Some will let you use their names and others may let you share their story and ask you to keep their identity confidential. Either way, there is great power in sharing your past success stories with prospects.

One last point on this is to make sure you don't share your success in a bragging, conceited way. The best way to approach this is to remember that people like to hear about themselves, not you. Sharing past successes should be presented as a win for your customer, not necessarily for you. They will get the message but it will come off much more professional and less pompous that way.

☞ **Your Attire:** You and your employees represent your business. People develop attitudes about your business based on what you and your employees wear at work. Obviously, dress appropriately for whatever your profession is.

A particular challenge today is young employees who follow the latest trends of tattoos, facial piercings, eccentric hair dying, etc. If you're in a business that needs to appeal to the conservative, that can be dangerous. It is always better to err on the side of conservatism. Unless, of course, the trends are appropriate for your business. If you have a business that caters to a younger audience then have your company attire cater to that. It's the same if you were to flip-flop it. A suit and a tie wouldn't be appropriate when working at a water park or running the service department at an auto dealership. Whoever your audience is, make sure you put enough thought into your company's attire. It is a marketing strategy and weapon.

☞ **Your Customer Service:** Your customer service presents you with a huge opportunity. I have not been in too many restaurants that try to discourage you from coming in to begin with, but I was at a Mexican restaurant waiting to be seated. I was checking over the menu to see how many varieties of rice and beans they had when I was nearly knocked over by a section on the bottom of the menu. It took up nearly one third of the menu. At other establishments, this section usually only takes up a small line on the very bottom of the menu.

This establishment was very different. This large section of the menu was called "Regulas de la casa," which in Spanish means, "Rules of the House." What is it with rules in a restaurant? I felt like I was a child again at my parents' dinner table on a night when they were entertaining dignitaries. Here are the rules:

1. Sorry, we do not offer separate or itemized checks.

2. Because we are a small restaurant, we will not seat you until all your party is present.

3. Minimum service per person: $4.00 per services. (So what if you spend less than $4.00, is it self serve?)

4. Items topped with sour cream or guacamole will not be hot. These are cold items.

5. Reservations not accepted.

6. We do not accept personal checks.

7. We reserve the right to refuse service to anyone.

8. Prices subject to change without notice.

9. No cigarette or pipe smoking.

And the last rules read, Fifteen percent gratuity added to parties of 6 or more, 18 percent on parties over 10. Man, these guys really have it down. They must know that with lousy service no one will want to tip anyway so they add it to your bill.

There was this final note on the menu, "Ask about our catering, gift certificates, and party platters." Are you kidding me? After this long list of restrictions you think I want to spend more money here? I am afraid to hear about the rules for catering. I can just imagine it, "Sorry, no deliveries." When this place opened up it was packed because it was the only Mexican food within 15 miles. Not too surprisingly, however, it is not very tough to get a table these days. The service is equal to the rules. It is absolutely pathetic, but the food is good. Just make sure you mind your manners, keep your napkin on your lap at all times, and never, never, put your elbows on the table. It is against the rules.

Here is another customer service story that is the complete opposite. I took my two-year-old and my wife to breakfast one morning at the local bagel shop, Big Apple Bagels. It is always crowded there. I had been there before on several occasions but not with any of my kids. The service is very friendly, almost a Mel's Diner feel from the old sitcom, "Alice." All the locals go there.

It started out a little rough though that day. My son, Josh, hit his head on the counter while we were ordering. He really smacked it. As we finished paying, with him still crying, the cashier gave him a lot of attention even though there was a line building up behind us. She reached down behind the counter and grabbed a little toy, a plastic Slinky. He stopped crying immediately and lit up like he just saw Santa Claus. It was great. This was not all.

We were sitting there enjoying our scrambled egg bagels when the owner of the business came over and asked how everything was. You know I was not used to this at a regular bagel shop. Usually you get your bagel and coffee and get out, or sit there uninterrupted while you read the paper. She was very sweet.

A few minutes later, after we chatted for a few minutes with her, she went to another table in the lobby and talked with the folks over there. Toward the end of our meal she returned with something in the palm of her hand. She reached out her hand and gave our son a chocolate gold coin. He went nuts. Not only does he love candy, but candy in gold wrapping was definitely a hit. She gave some as well to the kids at the table next to us. The kids' faces lit up, as did the parents. She was working the crowd and did a great job of it.

Remember this, when it comes to customer service, sometimes the difference between excellent customer service and poor customer service is just a few simple things that take a little bit of effort. And believe me, service is one marketing weapon that can make or break you very quickly.

☞ **Your Flexibility:** One of the biggest differences between an individual business person and a large corporation is the degree of flexibility each possesses. Here, the balance tips in favor of the small business. Because the small business has not indoctrinated numerous levels of management and a gigantic sales organization on the tactics and strategies of its marketing plan, it can make changes on the spot. It can be fast on its feet and can react to market changes, competitive ploys, undeveloped service niches, economic realities, new media, newsworthy events, and last minute offers.

Once a major advertiser was offered an unbelievably good media buy for one-tenth of its normal price. Because the offer did not fit into the company's "engraved-in gold-plan" and because the person to whom the offer was made had to check with so many bosses, the company turned down the offer. A tiny business then accepted it, a 30-second commercial just before the Super Bowl at a fraction of the cost. Due to flexibility, the giant corporation was unable to take advantage of the bargain. Speed and flexibility are the essence of guerrilla marketing.

Successful marketers are also inflexible in their marketing plan leaving room for adjustments and readjustments, when necessary. When a marketing weapon hits a home run, a guerrilla uses it more. When one bombs, they simply adjust and keep moving forward with what works.

☞ **Your Competitive Advantage:** Many of today's products and services are so similar to each other their only difference is their marketing. They try to woo new customers with jingles or special effects and fancy productions. These marketing devices are desperate solutions for people with limited imaginations. Your competitive advantages are seriously potent marketing weapons. If your product doubles the profitability of a company or grows hair on bald heads or attracts lifelong love partners you don't have to use special effects. The truth will do very nicely.

Perhaps you have many competitive advantages but the only ones that can be translated into instant profits are the marketable ones. A new kind of fabricating material, unless it's a dramatic advancement, will probably only bore your prospects. A toothpaste that eliminates plaque, cavities, and bad breath while whitening teeth at the same time can be marketed with the high expectation of success. The idea here is to identify your marketable competitive advantages, then stress them in all of our marketing. If you don't think you have any competitive advantages you've got to get some or you'll never compete with your full potential.

Nuts and Bolts of Assessing Your Competitive Advantages

1. Will your target market perceive this as an advantage?

2. Is this different from what your competitors offer?

3. Will people honestly benefit from this advantage?

4. Will they believe your statement about the advantage?

5. Does this advantage motivate them to buy now or soon?

Your Marketing Insight: In order for you to do everything we've talked about up to this point you'll need to work continually on marketing insight. I must say I'm impressed. I'm impressed that you're taking marketing seriously enough to buy this book and study it. Please don't stop here. The more you know about marketing, marketing weapons and strategies, the more the marketing world opens itself up to you.

I'm amazed at how many companies have succeeded with such lousy products or services because the company understood marketing. Just think how powerful you and your company can be with an outstanding product or service and outstanding marketing. Never stop learning. Continue to be on the cutting edge of marketing and you will always be a success. Marketing insight is so, so powerful.

☞ **Your Speed:** Every professional knows speed is very, very often a major key to success. We live in such a fast paced society where time has become a commodity. With the advent of computers, the Internet and technology, people expect things at warp speed. That carries into your business and your business dealings with your prospects and customers. Please see the importance of this.

☞ **Your Testimonials and Endorsements:** Guerrillas realize that trust is an endangered species these days. It takes a lot of time and money to persuade a prospect to trust you enough to give you his business. That is why guerrillas are so quick to use testimonials. They are free, relatively easy to get, and flexible enough to add potency to almost any marketing weapon. Best of all, they are believed. People believe testimonials.

The primary reason people do not buy from you is not price, it is not location, it is not service, it is usually trust. People are afraid of spending too much, of buying a lousy product, and of not getting the service they need. For these reasons, trust is the critical element in closing the sale.

If you are not a Fortune 500 company how do you persuade a new prospect to buy from you? Even if you are a Fortune 500 company there is no guarantee that your business will be around tomorrow. We have seen even Fortune 500 companies go out of business. Consumers have become increasingly wary of scams, empty promises, and products that do not bring satisfaction. Unfortunately, it is not always easy to distinguish a great product at a fair price from something that should be avoided. This weapon is a great way to generate trust and very few companies use it.

☞ **Your Reputation:** In order for you to use great testimonials and endorsements, you need a great reputation. In prior weapons, we've talked a lot about being believable. Customers buy your reputation. Follow through on your promises or those customers will spread much ill will about you and your company. It takes years to establish credibility and develop a good reputation. This only comes with consistency in all of your dealings. Be consistent with your message. Be consistent with your quality. Be consistent with your service. Be consistent with your follow through and follow up and you will flourish in your reputation. Your reputation is a very powerful marketing weapon as long as it's a good one.

Your Secret Shopper Program: To really understand how you are doing, it is essential that you spy on yourself and your own company. If you don't call your own company or really try to see your business from the customer's perspective, you may be absolutely floored when you do. It is much harder to gauge how you are doing when you are on the company side of the counter, so to speak. If you own a retail establishment, try sitting in the lobby and watching your employees interact with customers. You will obviously be pretending to work on something so as not to trigger some fake behavior by the employees just to impress you.

When I was in retail, I used to make a constant practice of observing employees. Employees have even a harder time than you at seeing the real picture. We used to have the goal of greeting each customer that walked into the Jamba Juice stores within five seconds. One day at our busiest location, I sat in the lobby and watched during the lunch hour, the busiest time of the day. I tallied every single customer who came into the store and made note if they were greeted or not. Out of 30 customers, only 18 were greeted. So after the rush, I asked the manager on duty how she thought they were doing with greetings. She said, well, I think we're doing great. I asked her out of 30 customers in the last half hour how many she thought were greeted. She replied that she thought they didn't miss anyone. I chuckled inside, almost a little sick to my stomach. So I very nicely pointed out that nearly half, only 50 percent were actually greeted, then took a moment to assess with her why so we could fix the problem right away.

Just because you or your employees think you're doing well, don't kid yourself. Take time to find out. Call centers observe employees all the time by listening in on random phone conversations. If you are at all serious about getting the real scoop on how your company is doing, you need a secret shopper plan in place. You can administer one of your own by choosing some regular customers to be your shoppers. Create a questionnaire for them to fill out during five different visits on five different days. Compensate them by giving them a discount on one of their visits or give them something of value from your business.

Secret shoppers work for retail businesses and also for service industries and online businesses. It's the same concept. If you don't have the time or desire to do one on your own, there are companies out there who do a great job for a nominal amount of money. The most popular concept right now is a service that helps you get your customers to complete a quick three-minute phone survey the very day they buy from you. The customer even has 30 seconds at the end to leave a voice message. The information is available to you within 24 hours via the web. You have real-time feedback from actual customers. You can narrow it down to what day and what time the customer came in and often who it was that helped them. This is an excellent tool for training purposes and one of the best companies I know for this is called Mindshare. Check out their website at www.mshare.net.

☞ **Your Designated Guerrilla Marketer:** The reality of running a small business means knowing exactly what you have got to do to be successful but not having enough time to do it. If you understand that Guerrilla Marketing can propel you into huge profitability but don't take the steps to activate it and maintain the process, your understanding of it is wasted.

Marketing can succeed only if time and energy are devoted to it regularly. Insight and understanding, savvy and skill, are useless unless action is taken and somebody is paying close attention to the marketing process. Maybe that somebody will be you. But perhaps you are too busy attending to the details of operations, finance, production, sales or service and if that is the case that somebody should be your designated Guerrilla Marketer, an individual who has the expertise, the interest, the desire and the time to mastermind your marketing.

Select that person from within your company or from the outside. There are lots of hired guns who would be delighted to eat, sleep and obsess over your marketing. Just be sure that you select somebody. Find someone who will approach the marketing function in true Guerrilla fashion with enthusiasm, with confidence, with high energy and a passion.

If the person currently running your marketing does not have those attributes you have got to get yourself another Guerrilla. Marketing, for all of its sophistication, is just like a little baby in that it needs constant attention and thrives best when it is nurtured and guided. Unless you and your designated Guerrilla provide the parenting your company will begin to fade from your customers and prospects' minds.

The companies that get into trouble are often those that establish marketing momentum and then move on to other things. Those other things should always include more and better marketing because marketing is a continuing connective process and not a series of disconnected events.

Your designated Guerrilla Marketer should be a person who knows how many marketing weapons are available to you, how many you can create right in your own office, which ones are free, what your competition is up to, and what kind of technology can help you.

Perhaps your designated Guerrilla will be your Marketing Director or Director of Sales. It might be a marketing consultant or the account supervisor at an ad agency. It might be you. Just be sure it is someone who shares your vision and absolutely loves every aspect of marketing. If you do not have a good marketer you are going to miss out on a lot of opportunities. You will constantly be in a position where your marketing must react rather than act and the spirit of your company will never come shining through.

If the person you need to shepherd your marketing does not quite know how to plan, launch, maintain and succeed with a Guerrilla Marketing attack you need to train them. The science, art and business of marketing can be learned. You do not have to be a born Guerrilla. There are books, seminars, lectures, courses, newsletters, internet sites and audio cds that can give a bright person more solid and realistic information about marketing than four years of study at a university that teaches Dark Ages tactics for companies with billion-dollar budgets.

How much time should your designated Guerrilla spend attending to the actions required by Guerrilla Marketing? The greatest amount of time will be necessary at the outset when the planning is done. Less time will be required during the launch phase when the weapons are actually fired and less time, but constant time, must be devoted as you sustain the attack. That time will be devoted to three tasks:

1. maintaining the marketing attack

2. tracking your marketing efforts, and

3. developing improved marketing.

Of the many reasons for business failures, an inability to market aggressively and consistently ranks right up near the top. When that happens, the finger of fault always points to you, the Franchisor.

You are now at the point where you can really impact your marketing. Make sure you or someone else in your company is your designated Guerrilla Marketer and you will succeed.

Your Timing: Very often, a company markets a great product or service to the appropriate target audience using superbly selected media but the marketing flops due to poor timing. For example, a ski bus announces its service during a year with no snow. A real estate firm produces a color brochure during a severely depressed year for real estate. Good ideas… terrible timing.

Time is not created equal. In order to get the most mileage from your marketing you must be keenly attuned to the right times and the wrong times. Consider these examples: You have created the perfect mailing package but it arrives too early in the week when your prospect is thinking of the week ahead or it is too late when your prospect is thinking of the upcoming weekend. The point: depending on the nature of your product or service, determine when your mailer should arrive.

You have a great product but a limited budget and a lot of competition so what do you do? Do your marketing when your competitors have eased up and you can gain the largest share of mind with the smallest share of marketing investment. Everybody receives Christmas catalogs in September or October right? Well, if you sent yours during June or July you would get people thinking of your company then and later on as well. It is a bit crazy, but if you explain why you are mailing it at that time it will make sense to your prospects. Naturally this approach can be applied to any holiday season and it is truly Guerrilla.

Keep abreast of current events by watching television, reading newspapers, and subscribing to publications in your industry. Then use that information to tie in your offerings with what is happening at that moment in history. Local news always does this. They feature stories that coincide with the show that precedes them that night.

Be careful not to launch a marketing weapon too soon before the bugs have been worked out of your new offerings or before sales people have been properly trained. Savvy retailers wait a month before having their grand openings. If they do not, customers will come flocking in and find untrained sales people, poorly stocked shelves, among other things, and they will be turned off. The timing of your marketing is big. Make sure that you get it right.

PROMOTIONAL MARKETING

NOW WE ARE going to move on to the promotional marketing weapons.

☞ **Your Word of Mouth Advertising:** As customers grow more cynical and media gets ever more crowded, word of mouth advertising becomes even more important. Most businesses in this country survive solely on word of mouth, making it their only marketing tool. Do you know businesses like this? Some people bristle at the suggestion of word of mouth advertising. After all, conventional wisdom says that you cannot buy word of mouth the way you can buy an ad. In fact, you can buy word of mouth marketing. The process is not as direct as calling up your ad agency, but an investment of time and money will eventually pay off in increased word of mouth exposure.

Understand that word of mouth marketing is a critical tool and realize that what appears to be word of mouth marketing is often the result of newspaper, magazine, radio and direct mail marketing. Often it is word of mouth that gets the credit and not the media. Do not delude yourself that you can hit it big with no media advertising at all. All successful Guerrillas use a combination of marketing weapons.

Truthfully, word of mouth marketing is the cumulative result of years of careful planning, media spending, and quality service by a guerrilla. In order to generate a referral or a testimonial from a loyal customer, you have got to take the time to set the stage. You can do a hundred little things to make your business attractive to a customer and the result will be a guerrilla's dream: a satisfied customer who sells for you. Who doesn't want that?

So how does one go about encouraging word of mouth advertising? How do you generate the buzz? Here is a way to give your customers an incentive to sell for you. Give your best customers ten brochures, each coded with their names. The brochure gives a new customer a $10.00 discount, making it attractive for someone to give you a try. As a reward to the loyal customer who distributes the brochures to his friends, give him a special bonus for every customer who brings in a coupon with his name on it; maybe $5.00 off. If you really want to be adventurous, offer the same deal to each of the new customers who comes in with the coupon. They too can give out ten more coupons and so on and so on.

I know a laser and skin center that incentivizes people by giving them a discount on their laser service. In the medical profession you cannot pay people to do advertising for you, but you can definitely give them gifts. For every referral people send to this laser clinic, they get a $25.00 gift certificate to use on any type of procedure of their choice. That is being creative. That is guerrilla marketing right there.

Business cards are also a great word of mouth tool. One accountant I know throws three into every piece of mail he sends out, and he invariably gets several new clients every year from people who happen to pass his card along. I have people asking me all the time who I use for my taxes or who I use for my yard or who I use for my swimming pool maintenance, and if I have a card and I am happy with that person, I will definitely give it out. I am sure you would too.

Give marketing materials to your new customers. Ad slicks, reviews, articles, and brochures remind them why they patronize you in the first place and it spurs word of mouth endorsements. The key is to ask for help. Perhaps the only people better equipped to talk about your company than you, are your best customers. Tell each one, "If you are really satisfied with our service or products, I would appreciate it if you would tell your friends."

By asking your customers to help you generate word of mouth, you remind them of how much they like your business and tell them exactly how they can help you. Satisfied customers will love to spread the word of mouth for you. Just ask them and remind them.

Follow the lead of subscription magazines during the Christmas season. Most magazines send out notices of a special gift-giving rate to introduce subscribers to the new magazine as a holiday gift. The following year they approach the recipient of the gift to renew the magazine on their own. The new customer probably would not have subscribed without the recommendation of their friend, who bought it for her in the first place. That is word of mouth. That happens to me all the time.

How about doing an extraordinary job for your customers? The single best way to generate word of mouth advertising is to amaze your customers on a regular basis. When I was in the Jamba Juice business we used to call that "wowing our customers." By over-delivering on even the smallest request, you will consistently make such an impact that your customers will want to share you with their friends.

How do we over-deliver? The secret of exceeding expectations is to find service areas of your business where a little extra attention from you will transfer into satisfaction for the customer. Here are a couple of examples. New cars are usually delivered to customers with near empty gas tanks. If I buy a new car and spend that much money, shouldn't I have a full tank of gas? Not necessarily. But, this is a very shortsighted way to start a relationship with a customer. Mitsubishi dealerships deliver cars with gas tanks full. This gesture probably costs them about $30.00 - $40.00 a car, but it certainly generates a positive feeling that often translates into a personal recommendation worth much more.

Remember this, guerrillas build their businesses by enlisting their customers as salespeople. What is it that you can do to over-deliver to your customers or clients? What is it that you can do to "wow" them and get them spreading the good word about you? Think about it.

☞ **Your Community Involvement:** An excellent way to create word of mouth is community involvement. The old adage that you can do well by doing good is definitely true for the guerrilla. Your business should be involved in the community because it's the right thing to do. It can also increase customer loyalty, sales, and profits. Customers want to give their business to people who care about them. Even if you can't possibly contact every prospect to let them know that you care about the local community, you can demonstrate it clearly through your company's actions.

What about Ben and Jerry's, the Body Shop, Readers' Digest, and dozens of other companies that have established themselves as good corporate citizens. By publicly supporting ventures that help their target markets, they've broken through the clutter and attracted attention for their products and their good deeds.

Nuts and Bolts of Generating Goodwill

- Sponsor a little league baseball team or basketball team.
- Regularly donate food to a local homeless shelter and volunteer to help deliver and serve it.

- Sponsor a charity basketball game between your staff and the local police or fire department.

  - This works especially well for businesses with a lot of public contact making it easier to sell a lot of tickets.

- Furnish your space with art by local artists. I see this at restaurants all the time.

- A hardware store trying to hold its own against a competitor like the local Home Depot could lend tools or donate supplies for a fixup senior citizens house event.

- Work with an organized social agency to help organize a block event.

- Donate your parking lot for kids to set up a car wash to raise money for their school sports teams and organizations.

- Sponsor a road race to raise money for a local charity.

  - If there isn't one in your local community, consider starting one yourself.

- Support your local police department's DARE program. Donate giveaway items like T-shirts with your logo and DARE message to students attending anti-drug presentations by the police.

There are hundreds and hundreds of ways that you can become involved with the community. It's simple. You just need to pick one and do it because you care. As mentioned before, sales and profits and customer loyalty will definitely follow.

☞ **Your Package and Labeling:** Do not overlook the power of your package and labeling. It is fashionable to be cynical about packaging these days. After the explosion of the packaged goods industry in the '60s and '70s, many consumers got turned off. Packages over-promised and became extravagant. They drove up the prices of the products without offering any added benefits. Even still, there is great value in carefully considering this important element so do not dismiss it too quickly.

Entire businesses have been built around packaging. Leggs is our favorite example. Here is an ordinary pair of pantyhose, brilliantly marketed in a low-cost, self-service package that revolutionized the way women buy pantyhose. The only thing they need to do now is figure out how to make pantyhose that do not run. But without the package, there would be no product.

Other products that have been built around their packaging include Paul Newman's salad dressing. Whoever thought to put the face of a movie star on a bottle of salad dressing? Well, it works. Tic-tacs is another unique way. What about Perrier bottled water, one of the first bottled water companies to bottle water? Softsoap, took soap from the bar to the bottle. What about Pez? My kids all love Pez candies.

And what about the Capri Sun bags? Whoever thought of putting juice in a bag? My kids drink those things all the time. There's Kentucky Fried Chicken's bucket, a bucket of chicken. These well-known products owe much of their success to their superior packaging. The product's identity is in the package.

Nuts and Bolts of Packaging

1. Your package should be easy for the retailer to handle and display on the store shelves. If you make it difficult for the retailer, he will not want to be bothered and will replace your product with somebody else's. Ask yourself whether or not your package is too tall to fit on the shelves or too

flimsy to stand up to being handled or too awkward to be arranged on the store shelf. If it is, you must redesign it. Make sure that your package is sturdy enough to stand up to the handling process. One glass company packages its products in a flimsy cardboard container, almost 15 percent of the goods are already broken when they reach the retailer, and another 5 percent of them break while on the store shelves. That leads to profit loss and generates bad will with the customer who tried to buy the product, but broke it in the process.

- Another thing, do not be afraid to make your packaging more expensive than your product. Perfume or other fantasy products sell because the package is the product. When Infocom started selling computer games, they packaged a 60-cent floppy disc in a $3.00 box. It made it easier for them to charge $40.00 for their product and the markup quickly translated into a very profitable strategy.

2. If you are selling by mail, take into consideration the cost of mailing the product with the packaging. If the packaging increases the postage necessary by too much, change the packaging. Another thing is that you cannot forget about the law when designing your package. There are strict regulations about package design, the product claims that you put on the packages and even the sizes of some packages. Do your homework or you might get stuck with a warehouse full of goods you cannot sell.

3. Your package should communicate your positioning distinctively. Experiment with different shapes, textures, colors and materials to find a niche. Most baking soda comes in an orange box because that is what Arm and

Hammer, the market dominator, uses. If a guerrilla intro-duced a new baking soda, the color of the box would be a critical decision. Look at products like flour or break-fast cereal or antiperspirant. Every product in a large cat-egory is packaged similarly. Break the rules a little bit and you might be able to grab a significant market share. GE did it with their air conditioners. They reduced the size of their package by taking out some of the packag-ing material. Then they stuck handles on the sides of the box, thereby transforming it from a product that a deliv-ery man would bring to your house to something you could buy and carry out of the store yourself.

Sometimes the package is the product. Take, for exam-ple, the Colgate toothpaste pump or the Capri Sun juice bags. When these products came on the market they were hailed as revolutionary. Why? The juice was still basically sugar water and the toothpaste was still the same stuff Col-gate had been selling for years. The packages made all the difference. They were so radically different that both were able to enter the market as virtually new products, so the package created the product. What about your product and your packaging? Take a strong look at it.

Nuts and Bolts of Package Design

1. The words, design, colors and materials all have to work together to inspire the confidence.

2. If the package is low quality, the customer will assume that the product is too.

3. The customer should be able to obtain enough informa-tion about what it is inside to make an educated buying decision.

4. The copy must outline the product's description and key selling points.

5. Do you need a window? Many products, especially kids' toys, profit greatly from showing the consumer exactly what is inside. That is powerful.

6. If you are considering using purchase displays, be sure that your package fits the standard sizes offered by the industry. This will save big money in the long run.

7. The package must fit into the overall identity of your company.

8. Your logo should be prominently displayed and your company theme and slogan boldly stated.

The best packages say pick me up. Once the consumer has your product in his hand, the battle for the sale is more than half over. Get it in their hands.

How much should your package weigh? People have expectations and you should take those into account. Bicycle helmets should feel light as a feather when lifted, while expensive software products are expected to be bulky and heavy. So do some tests. Test the product line, test shipping, test retailer acceptance and test consumer opinion. In marketing we need to test, test, test, time and time again.

☞ **Your Referral Program:** It doesn't matter what business you are in, it holds true that referral customers many times become your best customers. Too many people miss the opportunity to obtain referrals. It generally costs you nothing more than the effort to ask. Just ask for the referral. The best time to ask is when the customer is most excited about your product or service. This is generally right when they make the purchase. When you are consummating the sale, ask your customer who else could benefit from your service or product. Do not ask for a list of 10 or 20 names. Instead, make it simple like everything else we do in guerrilla marketing.

Be specific. Ask for three names or five names but not more than five. Those three to five names are golden. You may choose to have a formal referral retrieving process or just keep it causal. Many people think that it is not as easy to obtain referrals in a retail setting because it is not generally asked for. However, if you are in the laser and skin business you may offer a $25.00 voucher good toward any one of your services for each person the customer brings in. If you sell smoothies, you may offer the customer a free smoothie when they bring in a friend that has never been in before. Whatever your product or service, don't miss out on the goldmine of referrals. Just ask.

☞ **Your Frequent Buyer Program:** It's easy to get more referrals if you provide a frequent buyer program. Have you ever flown a particular airline in order to earn their frequent flier miles? Guerrillas can use that same technique to build long-term product loyalty. With competition as stiff as it is, anything you can do to keep a customer from trying an alternative helps you maintain your market share. A successful frequent buyer program can encourage people to stay with you without costing you a lot of money.

Another benefit of a frequent buyer program is that it helps you identify your most important customers. If 20 percent of your customers account for 80 percent or even 50 percent of your business, you want to watch those customers very closely. By introducing a frequent buyer program, your best customers are immediately singled out by your staff for special treatment. Be careful not to make the requirements for awards too stringent. If it is too hard to participate or if the prizes are not really worth the hassle, you will alienate your customers.

One example of this is in the early days of Jamba Juice we had a frequent buyer card. It was buy ten smoothies get one free. It was originally designed to only be used in the first few months, maybe even the first year of the business, but we ended up keeping it for two to three years, and after a while once we became established, we tried to take the program away, and what happened was we lost a lot of customers because they were so upset that they actually left and did not patronize us anymore. We learned from that experience that we needed to bring the card back.

If you are going to start a frequent buyer program, if it is temporary, make sure that you spell that out in the beginning. Let customers know it is only temporary and that at some point it will be going away. It is promotional. If you plan on keeping it for a long time, then let people know it is a long-term program.

Nuts and Bolts of Setting Up a Frequent Buyer Program

1. <u>What is your objective?</u> Are you trying to reach people who are already customers or are you trying to set up a continuity program to attract new business and attract your competition's clients to your company?

2. <u>What are the logistics of this?</u> Decide exactly what it is that will earn your customers the prizes or the points. Will they need to have a card stamped every time they buy or mail in a coupon to redeem their prize? Make sure you keep it as simple as possible.

3. <u>What exactly is their reward?</u> The prize or the reward has to be perceived by your customers as sufficiently valuable to induce action. At the same time, the rewards cannot be so lavish as to make the program a loser. The estimated increase in sales must offset the cost to make it a success.

4. How will you handle the fulfillment of the prizes? Make sure you can accommodate all of the people who joined the program. If you require proofs of purchase to redeem the gift, consider hiring a fulfillment house to process the orders and mail out the rewards. If customers have to wait too long for their reward, the program will backfire, creating more dissatisfied customers than loyal repeat buyers. Be careful with this. Make sure you think through your frequent buyer program before you set it up.

☞ Your Free Gifts: These are also referred to as advertising specialties and samples. Advertising specialties are items on which the imprinted name and sometimes the address, phone number, web site, and theme line of the advertiser appears. Examples are: ball point pens, scratch pads, mouse pads, briefcases, caps, t-shirts, screen savers, decals, bumper stickers, banners, lighters, coffee mugs, shopping bags, fanny packs, and, one of my favorites to receive, mini jump drives to store computer information. There are limitless things that you can use.

Why would you do this? Think of specialties to be the equivalent of billboards. That means they are great for reminding advertising. If it is a good useful gift, people will see your company name. Nike and all the big corporations spend millions of dollars in endorsements to get professional athletes to wear their free gifts. You can do this same thing on any level. It is the same concept. Get your name and logo out there.

Titan Pest Control in Anthem, Arizona, teamed up with the school PTA and created a four by four inch magnetic calendar for families to hang on the refrigerator. The calendar has important school dates on it along with the company logo and phone number. Guess where it's been all year? You got it, right on our refrigerator. Guess who I think of when I see a bug in my house? That's right,

Titan Pest Control. How much do you think the PTA paid? Nothing! It was a small investment for Titan because it was sent home with every student, all 800 of them, the first week of school. Talk about Guerrilla marketing. That was awesome.

I use the keychain that my auto mechanic friend gave me from Armstrong Automotive. Just three weeks ago, my other friend asked me if I knew a good mechanic. "Well, yes I do," I said. The next question of course was, "Have you got his number?" And there it was, right on my keychain. Armstrong just got a new customer from that keychain and it cost them about $.25 to make. That is the power of gift giving at work. What do you give out for free? Use free gifts and get your name out there. It works.

☞ Your Public Speaking Expertise: Everything we do in promotions is to get maximum exposure. One way to do that is to be a speaker at a club. I am sure the first club you are thinking of is the Chamber of Commerce. While this is a great place to give speeches it is only the beginning. There are hundreds of clubs and organizations out there that need lunchtime speakers. Find out who they are and where and when they meet. Prepare an informational presentation, not one that sells because you are going for exposure.

If you are in the service or manufacturing business and do not think this one is for you, think again. This can be a great avenue for almost any business, especially if it is out of the norm for your industry. It can be creative and create a lot of talk about your company.

Another key is to make sure you have something to leave with them, a brochure, some kind of video or audio brochure, or, at the very least, your business card. The main point is to get their information and their permission to put their name on your newsletter list. Offer to send them something for listening to your presentation.

This is where most people blow it. They go to events like this, this goes for mixers as well, and they only give out their card thinking that the person will call them right away. The truth is that most people will toss your card the next day. That's why it's important to get their information. It puts you in control of following up.

☛ **Your Publicity:** As you establish yourself in the community as an authority in your industry by speaking, it will help you get more publicity. The guerrilla already knows that word-of-mouth is the most powerful marketing weapon. One of the best ways to generate word-of-mouth is through publicity. The unbiased nature of stories in the press generates interest from consumers that you could never reach with advertising.

Understand this, the press needs your stories as much as you need to see them in print. Every day there are newspapers to fill, broadcasts to film, and radio shows to produce. Without stories like yours the newspapers would carry nothing but articles about wars in foreign countries. There are a number of great books about publicity and public relations, and many great guerrilla techniques that you can use to break through the clutter.

Nuts and Bolts of Publicity

1. Don't send material to everyone. A press release sent to Time Magazine is almost certain to be a waste of time. Pun intended! Instead, pick five or ten publications or media outlets that you'd really like to see your story appear in. Focus on them like a laser beam. Find out which editors have created stories similar to yours and go straight to them. And remember, for most businesses, a local story is better than a national one.

2. Break the rules. If you're not a PR professional, don't worry so much about appearing to be one. If you want to send a dozen bagels from your new bagel baker, go ahead. Some editors may frown, but at least you got

their attention. When I was in the Jamba Juice business we got so much free publicity from this. We would just show up at a radio station or a television station with free Smoothies for everyone there. We got invited to be on television all the time. We were on the radio all the time. We did this by promoting different events, but sometimes we just showed up and said, "Hey, here are free Smoothies for the group." Then a few months later when they were doing a special on Christmas treats, they'd call us in for one of our Christmas Smoothies. It was great publicity and it was free, except for the cost of the product.

3. Be persistent. Just because your story didn't get picked up this week, don't give up. You can probably come up with one newsworthy event every month. Every month send a press release to your target list of five or ten. Sooner or later it will work. When we were a new brand in Phoenix, Arizona, eight years ago, although we brought free Smoothies by, it took some time. People didn't know who we were. They were a little hesitant at first about drinking something we brought in, but after a little bit of time and much persistence, we got in. And now they call us!

4. Buy some PR, remembering, the smaller the paper, the better the odds. Most advertisers supporting small papers and radio stations will be happy to publicize your event if you're a regular advertiser. Talk with the ad representative about your chances of being covered.

5. The business owner who sends out several hundred press releases and then sits back and waits is probably not going to get a lot of return for his effort. Public relations takes a lot more ingenuity than that. Your press

release is a good place to start, but make sure you've done your homework.

- Make a list of all the publications you think might be interested in your product and research them.

- Find out what kinds of stories they tend to cover the most and who the key editors and writers are.

- Call the editorial offices and find out who should receive your materials and if there are any special requirements.

- Personalize your cover letter and show off your knowledge of the publication.

- Mention an article you've read or an issue you found particularly interesting.

  - People want to hear how good they are, so tell them.

- Make suggestions of where your story might run in the next issue.

- Most importantly, your press release must be newsworthy.

  - Why are you sending it?

  - What's so interesting about your product, service or store and why now?

- Your story has to be compelling.

- Make sure you've written your story clearly and with a minimum of hype.

- Editors read thousands of press releases and they're not going to bother with yours if it is clumsy or difficult to read.

Your public relations job does not end with the press release. Follow up with a phone call. Send them a gift. Ask the editor if she needs any more information to write the story. If you reach a dead end, don't despair. It frequently takes more than one effort to get the coverage you want. Send out releases on a regular basis and continue to follow them up. Persistence will pay off with a big headline or at least a valuable blurb that you can use to build credibility with your customers and prospects alike. Publicity is a great guerrilla-marketing weapon and most of it's generally free.

Your Take-One Box: Take advantage of people's natural curiosity. If you own a retail store and don't have a take-one box on the counter, you're missing a lucrative opportunity. Guerrillas never stop selling once the customer is in the store. They use flyers, inserts, and coupons displayed in take-one boxes to help close the sale. For instance, if you have an electronics store, print a brochure or flyer called Basics for Buying a Stereo System. Giving your customers something in writing that tells them about you and your product is a fundamental guerrilla tactic. Also, use the brochure to include your qualifications, testimonials from previous customers, and other information that will persuade prospects to buy from you.

Another way to do this is by visiting every store in your neighborhood and arranging to put a coupon or stack of coupons for your product on their counters. Of course you need to offer the same for them. You may offer to pay each store something, or consider offering your product or service for every resulting sale. You may trade out the space by letting them put coupons on your counter. A local Chinese take-out restaurant has a box with take-one inserts from an auto lube and oil business, an automobile tire dealer, Carvel Ice Cream and Sport Time USA, sitting on its counter.

Rest assured that the restaurant has coupons on the counters of each of those outlets as well.

Pay attention to the details, guerrillas. Have a professional design your coupon or flyer. If coupons are not eye-catching, nobody will take them out of the box. And don't scrimp on the box itself. Something transparent is usually best. If people can't see what they're picking up, they'll probably ignore it.

A more traditional approach to take-one inserts is found in local supermarkets. Everyone has seen the boxes mounted on supermarket walls by the doors filled with flyers, circulars, and booklets advertising a variety of items. There are companies that specialize in distributing take-one space in supermarkets. You can contact one of them and have your insert put in every supermarket in the country. Chances are, though, you are more interested in regional or local coverage and those same companies can sell you space by the region. Look them up in the Yellow Pages and call them about advertising only in your particular region.

What about non-retailers? Can they use take-one boxes? Well, they're primarily used by retailers to boost their sales but a guerrilla manufacturer can also use the same technique to boost his sales by providing his retailers with take-one boxes. For example, Apple faced a huge problem when it had to educate customers about their Newton computer way back when. By describing the salient features of the machine in a simple take-one brochure, they made it easier for their retail distributors to disseminate the information. Discuss with your retailers the advisability of using take-one boxes and inserts that you would provide at no charge. You'll find that most of them are more than happy to give it a try.

What about the next generation of take-one? The take-one concept has also gone high tech, just like everything else. There are now take-one dispensers on product shelves and on grocery carts.

Even inside the grocer's freezer. Even though the technology is more advanced, it's still not a very expensive advertising medium especially if you're selling goods to outlets like supermarkets, pharmacies or convenience stores. Act Media in Norwalk, Connecticut, is one company that specializes in both in-store advertising and high tech take-one.

Nuts and Bolts of Designing a Take-One Box

1. Lead with your product or service. Your headline should be bold and to the point. You've heard that a lot, haven't you? It's because it's so important. Every headline that you do should be bold and to the point. The message should be clear and cause people to stop, look and pick up the insert.

2. Make your mast head or logo the centerpiece. The insert should communicate the identity of your product and company. You have a split second to grab the customer's eye and a logo or mast head is an effective way of doing that.

3. Include a valuable offer. The insert should have a coupon or special offer as the main point. Talk about a special sale, a promotional deadline, or a special feature you offer. You must create a sense of urgency and the promise of benefit with your insert. There has to be a reason for someone to pick up your insert.

4. Use color and quality intelligently. The insert really has to stand out but clarity is more important than flashiness. Use high quality coated paper. Finally, give the customer something that will make her take you seriously. Include an easy way for the customer to reply to your offer. If you insert a coupon, make it obvious and easy to redeem.

☞ **Your Networking:** If I were to prioritize these promotional marketing weapons, this next one would rank near the top. Every guerrilla knows that the purpose of networking is to learn of people's problems so that the guerrilla can provide the correct solutions.

The effective marketer sees networking as socializing with a business purpose. Listen to this next concept very carefully. Read it again and again. Networking with the idea of selling is the wrong mindset. Do not waste your energy talking. Use it to listen instead. Give other people a chance to talk. If you do your networking with the right people, almost all of those people will be prospects.

One of the yardsticks by which you can measure your networking is the percentage of prospects that become clients. The higher the number, the better you are networking. Another yardstick to measure success is the amount of information gathered. The more you learn, the better you networked. One more measurement is generosity. The more you give, the better you network. Give something such as important information, concisely presented or a lead to a prospect for your prospect. The more your tidbit of information helps the person you told it to, the better you did your marketing.

Too often I attend networking events and see people going around handing out cards. That is not effective. I, of course, try to follow the advice I just gave about listening. If anything, you should be collecting cards to put people into your database so that you can contact them because, I can almost guarantee, they most likely will not contact you unless you use the tips above.

Look at networking as an honest and natural way to establish trust and nourish relationships. It is personal marketing in its rarest form. Many of the guerrilla marketing weapons are involved, your attire, your personality, your enthusiasm, and credibility, your neatness, and your smile, just to mention a few. Your job is simple. Ask questions. Hone in on the problems faced by the person's company. Probe by asking more questions. Tell your reasons if you are asked about your curiosity which is that your company markets solutions to many problems. Perhaps you can help this person who is becoming both a business contact and a friend.

To network effectively, you need a networking strategy. That's right, a networking strategy. It requires only three pieces of information and keeps you on target in selecting networking sessions and getting the most from them.

Nuts and Bolts of Networking

1. State the purpose of your networking, perhaps to learn the problems your company can solve.

2. List the items of value you will be giving away, maybe a piece of information of value to the people at the gathering.

3. Your strategy outlines the groups with whom you will network so that you know which invitations to seek and which to turn down.

It is better to enter a networking situation with this data than without it. Otherwise, you have a good chance of getting distracted by the sounds of other networkers blowing their own horns. Make sure you do not waste time joining peer networks unless you want to establish alliances. Go where the prospects are. If you are going to network, do it effectively. Plan for it. Have a goal and a strategy before attending any event.

☞ **Your Event Sponsoring:** Networking will help you discover opportunities for sponsoring events. Understand that you will obtain sales much slower from sponsoring Little League teams than you will from certain other marketing methods, but entrepreneurs report that sponsorship of events does help other methods of marketing take effect more quickly. There is no question that you will make sales because of it.

You will also gain credibility as you support your community. You'll cause people to feel good about you. Don't underestimate the power of favorable association. It's big. Sponsor a turkey race on Thanksgiving, toys for the homeless at Christmas, Little Leagues during the summer as well as other athletic events.

Sponsoring events works especially well when you have a product that is intended for the audience of the sponsored event. For example, a sporting goods store or a health food store sponsoring a marathon or a 10-K event. Be careful though. If there is not a good reason for you to sponsor teams or events, you probably shouldn't do it. Don't just do it for your ego, but if there is any connection at all, do it if you can. It will pay off as a long-term marketing strategy.

☞ **Your Specific Events – Sweepstakes and Contests:** People love to play games. Last year more than half of all Americans bought a lottery ticket and Ed McMann of the Publisher's Clearing House Sweepstakes generates several new million magazine subscriptions a year. For a small investment you can create a sweepstakes that will focus attention on your business. You will generate traffic in your store and encourage people to try your product and spawn word of mouth.

Sweepstakes really are a great guerrilla weapon but you will need to be careful. Mistakes can cost you money, time and even a brush with the law. There are critical differences between contest sweepstakes and lotteries so we will talk about those definitions. The most important thing to keep in mind is that private lotteries, sometimes referred to as raffles, are illegal in all 50 states and if you run one you will probably get shut down. The defining element of all three is that there is a prize. If you do not give away a prize that costs too much you've got little to worry about.

If there is a prize, the next issue is what lawyer's call consideration. Does it cost money to play? This can be tricky. Most states consider a purchase in your store to be a consideration. That means that collecting store receipts as entries is illegal. In some states just buying a stamp to mail in an entry can be called consideration so be really careful.

The final issue is chance. Lotteries are obviously games of chance. No one ever won the lottery because he was a genius. Games of skill like golf tournaments, spelling bees and jeopardy, are generally considered to be an entirely different category called, not surprisingly, games of skill.

Getting more specific about definitions, lotteries are games of chance that involve an entry fee. They are illegal. Sweepstakes are games of chance that make it clear that there is no purchase required. These are the most common promotions. Contests are games of skill that involve an entry fee. They are illegal in many states and often trickier to administer.

Nuts and Bolts of Successful Sweepstakes or Contests

1. Require people to enter your store to enter the sweepstakes. While you cannot require a purchase you can require people to walk all the way to the back of your store to enter the sweepstakes. If you are a manufacturer feel free to ask consumers to answer a bunch of questions that can only be found by reading your ads or studying your box.

2. Make the prize fantastic. Cash is not usually a good prize unless the amount is stupendous. Consider travel or sporting events, services like free car washes for a year or other publicity generating prizes. A prize awarded over time is usually cheaper for you and just as enticing

to the winner. Even better, make the prize an event. One radio station gives their sweepstakes winner the opportunity to host a station-sponsored concert at his high school. The concert generates news and every single student in the school becomes grateful to the station.

3. Make sure people think they have a chance to win. By adding a skill component to a contest like, "answer the following three questions," you can encourage people who think they never win anything to actually enter.

4. Require names, addresses, and phone numbers to enter. People are usually very forthcoming with data if you ask for it in the sweepstakes entry. Put all the names on your mailing list for future reference.

5. Publicize the winner. Invite the local paper to take photos, and send out press releases with quotes from the grateful winner.

☞ **Your Club Memberships:** Don't just be a sponsor of events and contests, be a joiner of clubs. Join civic clubs and community organizations. This is quite possibly your most important marketing tool. While you will be doing your duty as a member of the community, you will also make lots of contacts with people who can give you business and with people who will refer business to you. Make sure you join each club for the right reason. I really hope you don't just join things just to obtain business. In fact, if you do, your true motivation may be discovered causing you to lose business. But if you join to aid your fellow man, you most likely end up with important contacts. If you work hard for the community people will assume you work the same way in your business. The most effective marketing tool can be to join organizations.

I am sure you have heard that much business is conducted on golf courses. In fact, I personally would like to conduct more and more business on the golf course, but just as much business is conducted in meetings, over lunches, on tennis courts, at dinners, and over cocktails, with fellow members of a club. A true guerrilla puts as much effort into public relations as possible.

☞ **Your Partial Payment Plan:** Make it easy for customers to do business with you through partial payment plans. We live in an era where people love to defer payment. It has become almost a necessity these days. Car dealerships do it, furniture stores do it, electronics stores do it. Many high-ticket items are purchased this way because it takes the sting out of the high-ticket items. Oddly enough, even mortgage companies are doing it with interest-only loans. It's everywhere. If your competition offers payment plans or deferred payment options, you had better offer them as well.

☞ **Your Free Consultations:**

> *Nuts and Bolts of Consultations*
>
> There are five consulting rules to follow:
>
> 1. Do not make a sales presentation. That's right. People all over the place are giving free consultations a bad name because of this. Don't sell. You will have a chance later.
>
> 2. Stick to your time limit. If you offered a 30-minute consultation, offer to leave after 30 minutes or, if they are at your office, allow them to leave after 30 minutes. Your prospect may ask you to stay and continue your consultation and, if you'd like, that is fine. Otherwise, you are honor-bound to finish when you said you would.
>
>   a. You prove in a consultation your professionalism, your ability to listen, your ability to help your prospect, your liability, your enthusiasm, and your maturity in a potential buyer/seller relationship.

3. Prove how valuable you can be to your client. Do it with sincere, valuable help.

4. Ask questions and listen carefully to the answers. The idea is not to hold things back but to give freely. If what you give is valuable enough, you'll be sufficiently compensated down the road.

5. Make sure you follow up within 48 hours. I know you're busy and may even have other free consultations set up but, no matter what, you should thank the person for his time and restate the high points of the consultation. If you're not willing to follow up, you may be wasting your time during the consultation.

☞ **Your Free Seminars:** Guerrillas have learned that the more they give the more they receive. A free seminar is a free sample but it will amount to doing it only in a vacuum unless two key factors are present.

First, your free and parting information must be advertised so that you'll have a large group of prospects. Advertise in the newspaper, on the radio or on TV. Use direct mail and telemarketing. Post signs. Go for the free publicity that is readily available when you're offering a free seminar. Tell the truth in your ads as to the content of the seminar and try to attract honest prospects, not just warm bodies.

Secondly, be sure that either you or an associate can sell your offering to those prospects after the seminar is over. If possible, demonstrate your product or offering at your seminar. Even though your offering is free, people are giving up their time. They're traveling to attend your seminar and they have expectations based upon your ad. You must give them value in exchange. You must treat them as if they have paid to see you. And even if they don't buy from you make sure they still feel their time was well spent. Perhaps they'll buy from you later.

Most seminars are held at hotels or local libraries where facilities are readily available. However, if you have a store and you can work the space for a seminar, hold it. That will work best. Your prospects can learn where you are and what you sell. For instance, a decorating seminar in your furniture showroom is a natural. When conducted properly and with these two factors in mind, free seminars can be very powerful.

☞ **Your Free Demonstrations:** Free demonstrations can be given not only at seminars, but also in homes, at parties, in stores, at fairs and shows, in parks, at beaches, almost anywhere. People are attracted to small crowds. Remember, commotion equals promotion. You can feel free to use that anytime you'd like. See, I walk the talk. I give out free information as well you know.

Speaking again of free demonstrations, make sure you keep them at five minutes or less. Any longer and it should fall under the seminar category. Be prepared to sell and take orders immediately afterward. People who give seminars and demonstrations often have associates set up to accept customers' credit cards, checks, and, of course, cash. The person giving the demonstration or seminar is usually too busy answering questions to take orders, so make sure you get the rest of the sales opportunity organized with sufficient staff and equipment.

☞ **Your Free Samples:** Free sampling is a great and powerful marketing weapon. Sampling can launch you to success with a great product or put you straight out of business if it is not. Look at what sampling has done to the computer software world with the free AOL trials and free 30 day use of countless other software programs. They get you hooked with the free trial. I am sure you have received samples mailed to your home such as toothpaste, cereal, or shampoo. Most offerings can be sampled. But, of course, you will have to examine your product or service to see if it lends itself to sampling.

The first product that comes to mind when I think of sampling is a car. You obviously cannot give away a sample car but you can give away test drives. It works. Once they get you behind the wheel of a car that performs, it is tough not to want it.

Here is a service that is not so commonly sampled - massage. That is right! I was walking through a mall the other day and there were four or five massage therapists with white gloves on giving Chinese acupuncture neck and back massages. It was $12.00 for 15 minutes. In a mall, are you kidding me? I am not going to sit there with my face in a face cradle and let a guy massage my back. Oh, was I mistaken. The lady offered me a free sample. I sat down and I was sold. I did not get up until 15 minutes later when I happily gave them $12.00 plus a tip. What a great business to give a sample of.

What can you sample in your business? Just get creative. When you decide what it is, sample it everywhere your prospects are, especially if you are a new company. Get the word out.

Food businesses are, without a doubt, one of the easiest to sample. If I were trying to build sales in a restaurant or fast food business I would give out vouchers in whatever media fit my business for a free item or a free meal. If your product is that good, the people will come back.

Sampling is just one of the tools we used to build Jamba Juice. When we started out in Phoenix in 1997, we could barely get people to take the free sample because they did not know what a Smoothie was, let alone Jamba Juice. "What in the world is Jamba Juice?" they would say. Over the years, we sampled at every school we could think of, at football games, track meets, after school. We went to gyms, 10K and 5K races, and every sporting event we could think of. We went into office buildings with samples. We went to car dealerships. We showed up at the parks on a hot day. We were on downtown busy street corners during the day.

Get in front of the people. Get your product in their hands. Sample...sample...sample.

Here are some additional examples of sampling companies. In the early days of water beds, people considered the beds to be a fad. To overcome sales resistance to the new product, a retailer offered a free 30-night free in-home trial. The company would deliver and install the beds and then make a phone call 30 days later to see if his prospect wanted him to pick up the bed. Ninety-three percent of the people bought them. Sampling paid off.

Another entrepreneur was launching a newsletter. He advertised in magazines. He engaged in direct mail. Both got mediocre results. Then he mailed free sample copies to prospects. Instant success! Sampling came through. Incidentally, it cost him a total of $500.00 to execute sampling but he realized $7,000.00 in profits from the attempt. A third company was marketing large screen television sets of his own design. Very few people took the time to visit the showroom where it was displayed so he took out ads offering free home trials. Soon he had to discontinue the ads because the response was so great. Even better than the response to his trial offer was the fact that 90 percent of the respondents purchased from him after sampling.

Another sampling idea is this, a person who washed windows for commercial establishments frequently washed the windows of his prospects for free. This demonstrated his proficiency, his speed, and his method of working. It also netted him several large customers and it did not require any advertising to get started. I could go on for ever and ever with examples but I want you thinking about your product or service. If it is at all possible to allow your prospects to sample your offering, let them! Your sales will soar.

☛ **Your Special Events:** Guerrillas understand that entertaining is enhancing relationships and ultimately drives sales. Look for opportunities to have a special event. Special events get media coverage if you invite the media. So invite them. Have a grand re-opening. Have a party when you have a new product come out. Time the new product to come out on your business anniversary, on your birthday, whatever. If you create a reason and entice people to come, it is a great opportunity to demonstrate your product and create a long term relationship with current customers and prospects.

☛ **Your Trade Shows:** A trade show is the best way to reach the greatest number of real prospects all in the same place at the same time. If you handle it right, you can obtain enough contacts to generate a year's worth of orders by attending just one trade show, but that is not the real reason to go. Trade shows are perfect for establishing long-term relationships that will pay off for years and years to come. Even in this age of faxes and email, the personal contacts that come out of a trade show can last for years.

Unlike almost every other setting, the sole purpose of a trade show is to sell. The attendees expect you to offer them products, and the newer and more exciting the product, the better. This atmosphere of buyer curiosity and seller enthusiasm is perfect for the motivated guerrilla.

Nuts and Bolts of Trade Shows

1. Select the right trade show. Chances are there are hundreds of regional shows and national shows you could attend. In some industries, there are one or more relevant trade shows each week. Obviously, you cannot go to all of them. You have to take into consideration factors like, who is attending, how much it costs, how much lost time in the office it will cost you to attend, the

quality of the show and who the other exhibitors are, before deciding whether or not attending is worth your while.

2. Remember that your job begins way before the show starts. There is a lot to do before the show:

   a. Send invitations to all of your prospects to pick up a free product at your booth when they attend the show;

   b. Send people a show schedule and a map of the exhibit hall so they find you very easily;

   c. Send out an entry form for a contest that people can enter by visiting your booth at the show;

   d. Put out a press release telling about the show and your plans to exhibit. If you are a local business planning to attend a national show, this can be particularly effective.

   e. Work with show management. There are often special seminars, parties and mailing lists available to exhibitors.

3. Go to the show with a definite goal in mind. Know whether you plan to penetrate your existing market or expand into a new market. Know if you are going for sales or just for leads, without a goal a show can be overwhelming and a total waste of money. If you're not careful and focused you can spread your efforts too thin and end up with nothing.

4. Concentrate on the design of your display. You need to make sure that it blends with your marketing identity and your current marketing theme. It is an excellent idea, if you

can, to include a hands-on demonstration or something that people can handle. Studies show that people love to touch things. At the very least, have something you can give away, ideally a sample of your product. And remember, most people do not like to walk into a booth where they might feel trapped, so be sure that your booth has an open feel. It is possible to spend a small fortune on a booth but it is certainly not required. When you visit a trade show, find a booth you like and ask who designed it. Find out where they got it, how much it cost, etc.

5. Make sure that you have the right people staffing your booth. This is crucial. Experts say that profitability of a show is determined primarily by the quality of your people and how they work the booth. They must be personable and knowledgeable about your company and your product. They must also be empowered to make the sale and deal directly with customers. When someone is there to buy, you do not want your employee saying, "Well, I can't really place that order for you, let me take your name and number and I will have a sales person call you in a few days." The customer will take her business elsewhere. I have seen so many booths at trade shows where the people just sit there and stand there and do nothing. It is imperative to your success to have the right people staffing your booth. Your people need to wow the prospective customers.

   Some other considerations include: maybe renting a limo and offering it to your biggest buyers to use at their convenience during the days of the show.

6. Run a contest. Try giving away a large screen television set. In order to enter the contest people must visit your

booth and pick up a button on which is imprinted your logo and promotional message and also a number. Hire someone to walk around the show to write down the numbers of all the buttons they see being worn. The winner is selected from those numbers. Sunsoft used this technique to sell their batman videogame at a show; over 8,000 people were seen at the show wearing a button promoting the Sunsoft product. Sunsoft probably spent $3,000.00 for the television set and $1,000.00 for the buttons but the impact of the promotion was priceless. Even if only 10 people saw the button, they made 80,000 positive impressions with key buyers. Very creative.

With trade shows it is important that you focus on the critical 20. You will find at every trade show that 20 percent of the visitors account for 80 percent of your sales. Yes, even here the 80/20 rule applies so use it to your advantage. Twenty percent of the visitors account for 80 percent of your sales. It is critical that you qualify your leads.

Immediately on meeting someone in your booth, introduce yourself and start asking questions. You need to find out what they do, what they want, how much they plan to spend. Unqualified visitors should be treated kindly, given a brochure and invited to look around. After all, you never know when an unqualified visitor will get a new job. Qualified visitors, on the other hand, should be immediately given the first-class treatment; invite them to meet executives, ask them to sit down, if possible, setup an appointment for them to return and speak when the environment is not so crazy.

Before you get to the show, create a special box for the business cards of qualified prospects. Every night, enter those cards into your laptop computer or business diary. On the morning you return to your business from the show, output all the names to mailing labels and send every person you met at the show a personal mail-merge letter along with another brochure. You will be amazed at how few people bother to follow up at all. Even better, if you really want to have impact, send each person a hand-written thank you card.

Do not forget the media. Trade shows are vitally important to the media. This is the easiest way for them to cover the trends that affect an industry. An alert guerrilla makes sure that the pressroom is well stocked with his press releases, is certain to attend relevant press conferences, gets lists of press attendees for follow up and keeps an eagle eye out for any press that may wander buy. Get some media attention at these trade shows.

Do not be afraid to ask for advice. Go to a trade show as a visitor before investing money to run your own booth. It is really important to do research in this area. Visit other booths, preferably not direct competitors, and tell them that you will be exhibiting at the next show. Ask them what works. You can also call your trade association and ask for their insight. The Encyclopedia of Associations lists the names and addresses of virtually every trade association in the country. You can probably find a copy at your local library.

☞ **Your Trade Show Displays:** Some very successful entrepreneurs use only trade shows as their major method of marketing. They display and sell their wares at trade shows, exhibits and fairs. They realize that many serious prospects will attend these gatherings so they put all their efforts into exhibiting and selling their merchandise. This is not their only tool but one of their major focuses. The marketing plan of many guerrillas consists of appearances at four major shows or fairs plus circulars or brochures to be distributed at the shows. Nothing else. Nothing else is needed.

One way you can get started with trade shows is to go to your local library and look up the Trade Show and Convention Guide. You can also look them up on the web or order it directly from Bud Publications in New York.

Another great starting point is to get and read a copy of *Guerrilla Trade Show Selling: New Unconventional Weapons and Tactics to Meet More People, Get More Leads, and Close More Sales*. That is by Jay Levinson, Mark Smith, and Orville Ray Wilson. It is a phenomenal book.

At the show, there are a couple of different ways to display what you sell. The standard way involves renting a booth for several hundred dollars, setting up your display, and giving it your best. Another way is very guerrilla like in nature and a fine method for testing the efficacy of trade shows as a non-media marketing medium for you. It entails visiting a show, finding a display booth that offers merchandise compatible with yours, and negotiating with the exhibitor whereby you share a portion of the next booth she rents. That means you pay part of the rental fee, assume part of the sales responsibility, and allow your items to be displayed and sold alongside those of your new partner.

When you visit one or two shows you will learn about products that compete with, or complement, yours. You will also discover products that knock your socks off, products you would love to be involved with and companies that you would love to use as future marketing partners.

Attending shows you will learn the right way to display goods and the wrong way. You will pick up some great ideas for brochures, signs, and demonstrations. You will even learn from the mistakes of others, saving you time and money, and you will meet people who may be able to help you distribute what you sell if you really work it.

Here is the final key to being successful at trade shows. You must get people into your booth and talk to them. Do not just expect people to walk up to you. Be out in front of your booth, calling people over. Give something away for free to each person that passes by. Add them to your mailing list. You must be aggressive and not passive. You must really work it.

Nuts and Bolts of Increasing Visitors to Your Booth at Trade Shows

1. Hand out circulars. Hire someone, a particularly very sharp-looking person with a great personality, to distribute your flyers while walking through the show. The cost to hire the person will be about $75.00 and for that they will pass out as many as 5,000 circulars, all inviting people to come to your booth.

2. A second way is to give away brochures. Because brochures are more costly then circulars you will not want to give as many away so distribute them at your booth only. This is a great way to get them into the hands of interested people.

3. Demonstrate your goods to those prospects who are in a buying mood. You can demonstrate your offerings to large groups of people. Since your competitors will probably be at the show too, you will have a great opportunity to focus on the advantages of your products.

4. Offer free samples. Rarely will you find a more ideal opportunity to give samples to so many potential customers. If it is possible, let people sample your merchandise.

TELEPHONE MARKETING WEAPONS

☞ **Your Toll Free Number:** Guerrillas make it easy for customers to call them by offering an 800 number. According to AT&T, prospects are seven times as likely to phone if the call is toll free. When 800 numbers were first introduced they made mail orders possible. Today they have become so ever-present that running a business almost requires one. You do not need to be a huge company to benefit from a toll free service. If your business attracts customers from more than one area code calling area, a 1 800 number must be seriously considered. Companies are now starting to install toll free fax machines, further encouraging their customers to contact them.

Advice about obtaining a unique and cool phone number is this: Unless you can get a custom number that is a complete keyword or phrase like 1 800 SOFTWARE or 1 800 FLOWERS, stay away from clever combinations like 1 800 777 1234. People think they will remember them and then forget. It is better to have a number that they have to write down. While using a clever pneumonic like 800 FLOWERS can make your business, be sure you use a word that people know how to spell easily. One company that makes water purifiers advertises their phone number as 1 800 BRITA44 – Brita4. And 1 800 GUERRILLA would be a bad idea because most people do not remember how to spell guerrilla.

One accounting firm in Houston, Texas, set up an 800 number that people could call to get information about taxes. The number is 800 4REFUND. Since introducing the number the firm has tripled in size. Go ahead and get creative with your phone number if possible. Just remember to keep it simple.

☞ **Your Telemarketing Script:** Studies in varied industries consistently reveal that a memorized presentation always produces better results than the same presentation from an outline. It may be more humanistic to let the caller use his or her own words but few callers have the ability to summon the right ones. Gone are the days when it was recommended the caller use an outline or a thought flow as they used to be called. It is true however, that the more naturally conversant one sounds, the more sales one will make and that takes practice.

Naturally, much of what you say will be in response to what the person being called says but the best telemarketers are in full control of the call. They stay in control by asking questions, directing the conversation toward the customer's needs. If you are comfortable using an outline to structure your phone presentations, be sure to heed the following guidelines. If the outline is longer than one page, you should try to streamline it. An outline does create a structure for your thoughts and ideas and it keeps the call on track when the person at the other end redirects it. So, if you do work from an outline, against my recommendation, it is a good idea to write the script of a phone call. After you write the script you should do three things.

Nuts and Bolts of Testing Your Telemarketing Script

1. You should record it and listen to it so you can hear what it sounds like;

2. Make sure the recorded script sounds like a conversation and not like an ad. Leave room for the person being called to talk; and

3. Make it a point not to restate the script but to rephrase it.

☞ **Your Greetings – Hello and Goodbye:** As simple as this may seem, do not underestimate the power of how you, and everyone in your entire company, greet your prospects and customers. Remember, marketing is any form of contact you or anyone in your company has with any part of the public.

One of the best companies I know at this is Freedom Marketing, a marketing distribution company. They specialize in door hanger advertising and distribution in Phoenix and Las Vegas. They answer their phone better than most companies I know. The line they use is "It's a great day at Freedom Marketing, how can I help you?" It's great. It's not only what they say, but how they say it. Call them. Here's the number, write this down 602 258 6400. Now don't just hang up. You might as well make their day by telling them you called just to hear how they answer the phone. While you're at it, you may want to find out about their advertising distribution services.

There are few places you can walk into these days and get a sincere greeting. And believe it or not, most people really do place a lot of importance on being greeted, not only greeted promptly, but enthusiastically. Here's another example.

About a year ago a Cold Stone Creamery ice cream store opened up near my home. I love ice cream, especially Cold Stone ice cream. This particular location was owned and operated by a franchisee. It was a family-owned business. We took the kids over during the grand opening week to celebrate our favorite ice cream place. Not only was the ice cream as good as usual, but the service was amazing.

When anyone walked in the door the crew of about four kids always yelled out "Hi, welcome to Cold Stone," with so much enthusiasm it almost knocked me over. Wow, I thought, this place is going to do a lot of business. There were smiles on the employees' faces and you could tell that they were having fun. Upbeat music was playing and they even sang a song every time you gave them a tip. This place was really into entertaining. We go back often.

If you really want to impact your business, no matter what kind of business you are in, show your enthusiasm with every single hello and goodbye. Make sure you and your employees treat every customer as if you had just started your business. Remember that enthusiasm you had right at the beginning? Yes, it does take work and it takes reminding your employees over and over again, but it does make a difference, and it will pay off all the way to the bank.

☞ **Your On-Hold Selling:** Don't you hate being put on hold when you call someone? I hate it, drives me absolutely nuts. I usually go by the 30 second rule. If someone puts me on hold or call waiting for more than 30 seconds, I hang up. The point is this: it really shows disrespect for the customer and it is a waste of time. But, as we all know, it cannot always be avoided.

How can a guerrilla keep an on-hold customer from hanging up, or even better, make them happy? Studies have shown that music on hold increases the amount of time people will wait. The tough trick is choosing a type of music that is appropriate for all customers. Radio stations can be unpredictable and no one wants to hear a screaming car ad while they wait. And, worst of all are those tinny digital loop recordings of Beethoven.

Microsoft Corporation receives tens of thousands of tech support calls everyday, most of which are on hold at one point or another. They solved the music on hold problem by hiring their own disc jockey who plays music and gives traffic updates and to appraise customers of how long the wait is on each line. Microsoft reports that the people are willing to wait nearly twice as long if they know where they stand.

A less expensive alternative is hiring a company like Musac or AEI to provide cds. They offer a wide variety of cds, not just elevator music. If you are going to play music, it is a good idea to interrupt with a voice every now and then, which tells customers that their calls are important to you and that you will be right with them. You can even get creative with this and say something other than that.

While the music is a good distraction, it will not keep people from thinking you have forgotten about them. You need to break up their time on the hold with a variety of things that will keep their attention. The last thing you want is for them to hang up. An aggressive guerrilla will not stop with music, she will provide information. You can create a five minute, endless tape that gives listeners news about your products or about your specials.

One guerrilla I know puts a secret discount on hold. Tell the operator that today the on hold discount is 4 percent with any order over $100.00. It is our way of saying thank you for waiting. How clever is that? If you hear it and mention it to the operator, you get the discount and the customer feels great about the two or three minutes they spent on hold.

There is a comedy club in New Orleans that uses a tape of some of its best comedians when it puts people on hold. It is so funny, there have been instances of people asking to be put back on hold. Get creative with your message on hold system and look at it more as selling on hold, than a waiting on hold.

MINI-MEDIA MARKETING WEAPONS

☞ **Your Business Card:** One of the least expensive, highest impact tools you can use to market yourself is your business card. Every business, from the largest conglomerate to the tiniest guerrilla, uses the same materials in creating a card. If you think of your business card as a chance to break through the clutter, you'll definitely distinguish yourself and your business.

At the very least, your card should include your name, company name, address, phone and fax number, and – write this one down – your positioning statement. This statement can be your slogan. For example, "You can't buy a better hospital crib," or a short description of what your company does, like, "Innovative marketing techniques for shoe stores."

You'd be amazed at how often people look at a business card with absolutely no recollection of who you are or what you do. I'm sure you've probably done the same thing with business cards. One large company, acting like a guerrilla, might put its executives' home phone numbers on their business cards. If you're trying to establish personal service, especially in an industry where speed counts, you can definitely build trust by including those types of things.

Never cut corners when producing your card. Use the very best paper you can afford and make sure it is professionally designed.

Having a local printer design your card is very shortsighted. In this era of desktop design, you can probably find a topnotch designer to do the work for just a few hundred dollars. Don't be cheap with your business card. There are tremendous opportunities to dress your card up to make it more useful and give it more impact.

One thing to remember is that you can use the back of your card. It costs very little and, if you don't use the back, it's just wasted space. A joke and novelty shop gives away a business card that has the following words emblazoned across the back: Another form of identification. Lots of their customers carry it in their wallet just waiting for a rental car clerk to ask for it. Wouldn't you rather have your card in a customer's wallet than in the trash? Be creative like that.

An info card is an ingenious new print product that lets you create a business card sized brochure. Maybe you've seen some examples of these before. You can include as many as eight panels of type giving you plenty of room to include lots of useful information.

Nuts and Bolts of What to Include on Your Business Card

1. Describe your business with a tag line.

2. You may want to include your price list.

3. Detail what your services are. It has much more impact if you give somebody your business card that tells what you do and what your services are than just your name, address, and phone number.

4. You may want to include a map of how to find your place of business.

5. You may give lists of toll-free 800 numbers or tourist information for their benefit.

6. You may want to profile key employees with a small bio about them.

7. Tell the success story of someone who has used your product.

8. Feature photographs of products, your office, or employees.

9. You might want to include quotes or jokes people might enjoy carrying around.

10. If you have a retail business, consider turning your business card into a frequent customer discount card. Some stores give a 10 percent discount to any customer who presents the manager's business card at the cash register.

11. You need to think of your card as a mini-billboard for your company. If you're a contractor, put them in the mailboxes of people in your neighborhood. Drop them into outbound mail. Hand them to everyone attending a meeting. If you've got something neat on the back it's easy to say, "Here's a list of 800 numbers you might need while you travel." Try using your business card as an active selling tool.

Print a double-sided card and on one side print the phrase "Present this card for" and leave a blank. Whenever you talk to a prospect, fill in the blank. For example, if you're a representative for a printing firm, you may come across a prospect who wishes that she could print her brochure more efficiently. Fill out the back of your card, present this card for a 10 percent discount on your next run of corporate brochures. This is a very personal offer tailored directly to the prospect's needs.

☞ **Your Letterhead:** Make your letterhead work for you. Many companies overlook the importance of their stationery or letterhead. Designing it seems like a simple enough task because we've all seen letterhead from thousands of companies. So just how hard can it be to get it right? Well, fortunately for guerrillas, most of their competitors do not even use one-tenth of the potential of their letterhead. A guerrilla has a real opportunity to create an alternative that delivers the impact needed to make more sales which generally make more profit.

First you need to remember that your stationery acts as your stand-in when you can not make a personal appearance. It should be as well dressed as you would be for an important meeting. Use the most expensive paper you can afford and stay away from colors. You might want to use white or a neutral color. Also letterhead should feature your name, address, phone number, fax number and email addresses. Simple enough, right? And remember this, it should also include your one sentence positioning statement. How often do you see that on letterhead? That is right, not very often.

A positioning statement does two things for you. First, it helps ensure that the reader of the letter understands the position of your company and, secondly, it reminds the busy reader exactly who you are.

In addition to a positioning statement, many guerrillas have turned their letterhead into mini brochures. List the full range of service that you offer. For example, if your mail receiving business also does typing put it on your letterhead. Let people know what you do. This is your opportunity.

Here is more food for thought. It is more than just your letterhead. You may also give some thought to what you put into the envelope along with your stationary. Many businesses have found that inserting a business card or a Rolodex card is a very low cost way to get their name and number into the hands of prospects.

Think about inserting something into every piece of mail that leaves your office, not just the direct mail letters. One business includes a business card with every check they mail out when they pay the bills. A carwash inserts a coupon good for $2.00 off every wash while the people at M&M frequently drop a coupon for a free pound of M&Ms in every letter they send to a customer. I want a letter from M&Ms. Stationery can be very powerful.

☞ **Your Banners and Signs:** Do not overlook the value of banners and signs in positioning your business to generate traffic. If you are located on a main freeway as many as 50,000 people may drive by your door on an average day. An effective sign can make a huge difference. L.A. is filled with businesses that have turned their buildings into huge signs. I am sure you have seen many of them. There are restaurants shaped like hot dogs, car washes shaped like whales instantly communicating their position to the consumer.

Nuts and Bolts for the Use of Signs

1. Proofread it exhaustively. Check and double check and triple check spelling. Mistakes happen often and they are a real turnoff to consumers.

2. Make a sign you can commit to. Spend enough money to make a great sign, then leave it alone. Do it right the first time.

3. Keep the message short. Drivers only have a few seconds to read your sign so stick with ten words or less, six is even better.

   a. On the way to the recording studio yesterday I remember looking at several billboards. One caught my eye but as I was reading through it I never figured out what it was because it was too wordy and the words were too small. I thought that was pretty funny because I was on my way to talk about this. It is really important to keep that message short.

b. You may want to look at effective billboards in your own community and use them as a model but make them slightly different. You will notice that those that are colorful with few words catch your eye.

4. Whenever possible, use lights on your signs and use flags on your banners. Make sure the zoning regulations permit signs or banners then make the biggest, most obvious sign the regulations will allow. Make sure you check in with the city and get that sign permit first.

5. "Going Out of Business" is not a useful slogan for a guerrilla trying to build a business. Please do not use this tactic. Do not try and trick your customers. You need to be honest so please do not use the, "Going out of Business" unless you actually are.

6. A low-cost way to attract attention is to string multi-colored flags, you know the kind that car dealers use, or rent a search light. People love to come to a special event even if the only thing special about it is that you have strung flags or rented a search light. If you can get neighborhood businesses to join in you can create a special event in your business district or out in your parking lot. String a banner across the street, put tables out on the sidewalks and create a bazaar. This is a great way to attract new prospects.

a. This even works for drycleaners. Serve mini hot dogs as a refreshment and offer discounted cleaning to anyone who spills mustard all over himself.

7. A great technique for small businesses on busy thoroughfares — rent-a-sign that lets you change the letters daily. If you are clever enough, your daily message to commuters

can be a regular part of their day and you can actually have people looking forward to seeing your sign. That is a big first step to establishing a relationship and turning people into customers.

Your Outdoor Signs: How many times have you been looking for a place and you end up driving around and around, getting so frustrated you can hardly stand it? I know I have many, many, many times. Generally, it's because I can't see the sign. It is either poorly designed or poorly located. If you have an office or a retail location or a place of business that people visit, please don't do this to your customers. Please, this will kill your business faster and easier than anything else.

Again, if you have a long business name, it will be hard to make it fit effectively on your outdoor signage. Use a short name whenever possible. Keep your signs simple. When possible, use colors that contrast with the building the sign goes on. Too often I see signs that blend in with the face of the building. Those signs could have double or triple the impact by changing the color or by putting a colored background behind it if you can't change the color of your sign.

Too often, people add unnecessary graphics, which also takes away from the sign itself, and makes it cluttered. Remember, the people who need to see your signs are looking for you for the first time or not looking for you at all. That is another good reason to use lighted signs whenever possible. Keep them lit, even after your business hours. Your sign is like a billboard even when you aren't open. Make it easy for your customers and prospects to find you with a solid, great-looking outdoor sign.

Your Outdoor Ads: Outdoor Ads differs from Outdoor Signs. Most advertisers worry about clutter wondering how their ads will stand out in the sea of commercials. Outdoor advertisers have a different problem. They're competing with trees, street signs and beautiful sunsets, which is a little more challenging. The lack of clutter in outdoor advertising is one of its biggest advantages. The other is boredom. People sitting in traffic or waiting for a bus have nothing to do. Their brains are hungry for information. The first billboard in sight burns itself into the prospect's mind. It's a home run.

Since childhood, we've been conditioned to believe that only huge companies like Marlboro, Seagram's and 7-Up can afford billboards. That's exactly the mentality the resourceful guerrilla is counting on. Billboards convey a sense of stability and give your message a larger than life appearance. A well-placed, well-designed billboard does wonders for your credibility and for your sales.

Several stores have built their entire business around billboards. Waldrug located in rural South Dakota has billboards running for hundreds of miles in each direction. By the time the driver gets to Waldrug, anyone who's curious, hungry, or just in need of one of their free glasses of ice cold water, makes sure to stop. At last count, Waldrug was doing several million dollars a year in sales.

A fledging computer software company bought billboard space between the airport and the convention center in Chicago during the annual consumer electronic show. Every buyer who attended the show saw the billboard. With one billboard, which probably cost about $5,000.00, Spinnaker made themselves the focus of the tradeshow and created a heavy-hitting impression.

You can do the same with the Super Bowl. Everybody knows a year in advance where and when the Super Bowl is going to occur. Buy a billboard on the major highway leading to the football stadium. Over 70,000 consumers along with all the journalists attending the game, will see your message.

Billboards don't move. This means that your message is guaranteed to hit the same commuter every day at about the same time. As every guerrilla knows, repetition is the secret to advertising success and billboards deliver repetition, repetition, repetition. Properly used, your billboard can be a call to action leading directly to sales.

Ideally, the two most important words on your billboard are, "Next Exit" or "Turn Here." For example, a new store in the San Francisco Bay area that did not have enough money to advertise in more traditional media was able to afford a long-term contract for just one billboard. That billboard, fortunately, was able to contain the words Next Exit. Success came rapidly and overwhelmingly. Of course, the store had to do everything else right to succeed and it did, but the billboard gets most of the credit for increasing in-store traffic. If you can't use those two magic words, these three words also work well, "Two Miles Ahead" or "Three Miles Ahead." Use those as directionals.

As great as they are, it is so important to understand that you can't do the entire marketing job with billboards alone. But, of course, there are notable exceptions. A bedroom furniture store in San Jose not only had a hard to find location but also suffered from a willful lack of funds. However, the store did have the good fortune to be located near a billboard placed just before its freeway exit. So the store rented it. The billboard read, "Take a peek in the bedroom. Next Exit," and eventually won over so many impulse drivers, that the store was able to expand its marketing to include television and eventually became the leading store of its kind in the nation. It all started with one lonely but very hard working billboard.

Another furniture store used a billboard to spice up its slower months. During the summer months, this store held a promotion and sung its praises on the radio, the store's usual medium. It also added a downtown billboard in a very good location. Even though the billboard was only rentable for one month, it helped make the promotion a success turning the normally slow July into the store's most profitable month.

What about billboard pricing? Billboards are sold in a way similar to TV shows. They're given a rating based on the number of cars that will be exposed to the billboard in a one-month period. 3M, one of the largest billboard companies in the country, relies on the government to provide them with what they call their daily effective circulation, a fancy term for the number of cars that pass by the billboard every day.

Obviously, high traffic billboards cost more than out-of-the-way ones. In addition to traditional outdoor companies, which own thousands of billboards, there are smaller mom and pop operations. You also have the option of directing and maintaining your own billboard. Look in the Yellow Pages under Advertising - Outdoor. The listings will give you a good idea of the local versus national companies that broker the advertising in your area.

The price of billboards varies widely depending upon their location and whether you want to advertise on a superhighway or on a simple, local back road. To give you a rough comparison: it costs between $15,000.00 and $25,000.00 a month to advertise on a billboard by the Lincoln Tunnel in New York City. That's just about the top of the line. In Chicago, a highway billboard would cost between $2,500.00 and $6,000.00 a month so it does vary and it's worth checking into.

If you don't want to use billboards there are alternatives. There's more to outdoor advertising than just large billboards. Most cities offer all sorts of opportunities including advertising on bus shelters and subways and on benches. Airports also offer indoor ads that work just like billboards. Some smaller communities even offer advertising on their parking meters. And don't forget about shopping mall displays, taxicab displays and telephone kiosks. Some places even offer billboard space in bathrooms. Every bathroom stall or the wall of many men's bathrooms has a billboard. You've got to admit it's a captive audience.

Bus shelter ads are a relatively inexpensive way to make a lot of noise. New Yorker's may be an eagle sensor group and they're quick to believe that anyone who is advertising in New York is advertising everywhere. Since most of the media is located in New York, an aggressive bus shelter campaign in Manhattan can translate into word of mouth and buzz nationwide.

In one of my businesses, we used to use bus shelters quite often but we used them as directionals and unless you have a huge budget, you can't brand with bus shelters and billboards alone. Like billboards, if you can find one that's located right before your turn or a short distance around the corner and you can use it as a directional, it can be very effective and surprisingly inexpensive.

Subway advertising can also be an effective tool, especially if your business is near a subway stop. Kennedy Studios, a chain of framing shops in Boston, uses this medium extensively. They advertise the subway stop for each of their stores along with clever stories and copy. When Kennedy started advertising on the subway they had far fewer stores than they have today so it's working. Bus shelters, subway ads, and airport signs give you more than a split second to convey your message.

As with a billboard, you still have to get the prospect's attention with a catchy headline or graphic. And now that your audience isn't speeding by in a car, feel free to make your point with as much text as you need. Someone waiting for a bus has at least ten full minutes to read your ad.

A proven technique for use in the subways is take-one pads. Attach a pad of tear-off flyers to your ad that people can take with them. Use your ad to attract attention and your take-one flyer to make an offer. Many of the firms that sell subway advertising will maintain your ad, checking the signs daily to make sure the take-one pads are full. The advantage of these pads is obvious. The person sees your ad on the subway, likes what you have to say, and takes a coupon. This call-to-action can translate directly into sales.

Nuts and Bolts of Negotiating a Billboard Contract

1. Never accept the published rate without negotiating for a lower price. As a guerrilla marketer, you know that you never pay full price. You can often save 15 percent to 25 percent if you will negotiate.

   a. I went out to dinner with my wife and her parents. We were in this little boutique-type store and my wife saw a picture that she really wanted. It was pressed flowers in a nice frame. Yeah, it was really cute but it was $80.00. I'm like, "Honey, do you know how many things you already have like this?" It really didn't matter to her, so I asked the sales lady, "Isn't there any way this might be on sale or you could give me a discount?" The sales lady said, "Well, it's too bad you weren't here three days ago. You just missed the sale." I looked at my wife and smiled as I said to the clerk, "Well, who's the owner of this place?" She said, "She just walked out the door. Her name is Jan." I said, "Where did she go?" The clerk replied, "I don't know. She just went that way," and pointed to the door. I said, "Hold on for just a second," and I went out and found Jan outside. I apologized for interrupting her and explained that I knew my request was going to sound strange. She listened respectfully. I told her that I happened to be in Phoenix last week during the 20 percent off sale but that I had missed out on it. I explained that my wife really wanted that picture. I asked if she could give us the sale price. She smiled and winked and she said, "You know, we could probably do that." I saved $16.00. Not only did I save some money, I also got a happy wife. My point is, no matter where you are, it's always worth asking if you can barter or negotiate on price. Sometimes you'll win, sometimes you won't, but it never hurts to ask.

2. Negotiate to shorten the length of the billboard contract. They say 12 months but you may be able to get it for six or even less. It just depends on the demand.

3. Buy at the end of the month. Billboard firms have quotas and often offer attractive discounts and incentives like many other sales companies. Realize that the winter is off-season in most states and you can save up to 50 percent sometimes. When public service billboards start to spring up that's your buying signal. There's empty space and deals are being made. Remnant space is a problem with billboards. Tell the billboard company you're interested but quite patient.

4. Ask for extra posters once you intend to buy. Once a billboard is being printed, the incremental cost for additional posters is small. You can place your own billboard on the side of your own building. Look for the billboard co-op funds from manufacturers with whom you deal. Some guerrillas cover 100 percent of the cost that way.

Nuts and Bolts of Designing a Billboard

1. Don't use more than six words. More than six takes too long to read. Keep the concept simple. Billboards are no

place to discuss frequent buyer programs, graduated rebates, and computer operating systems, et cetera.

2. Give the person driving by one large graphic on which he can concentrate, one that will really draw attention.

3. Make sure the type is clear and easy to read. Be sure the words are large. A person driving by does not have time to read small type. Don't waste your money with this.

4. Make sure the billboard is illuminated, especially if it receives a lot of drive-by traffic at night. There's a lot of advertising to be done at night. Make sure it's lit.

Nuts and Bolts for What to Include and What Not to Include on a Billboard

1. An easy to remember phone number. Make it big.

2. Something that moves. Billboards that have something that moves or that is three-dimensional really catch people's attention.

3. You may use a smoke-generating machine, a testimonial, a vivid photograph, your slogan, a giant coupon, or a specific call to action, like next exit, which is our favorite.

4. The one thing you don't want to do is put a photo of you or anyone in your family. I'm sorry. I don't want to hurt your feelings. For a billboard, you need to resist the temptation to make yourself famous. You need to put up words and calls to action on your billboard.

☞ **Your Indoor Signs:** Many guerrillas forget that the most important moment for any marketer is when the cash register rings. Having a store full of prospects may look good but it does not increase your profits. Getting the customer in the store is not enough. You have to close the sale.

Guerrillas, true guerrillas, use point of purchase displays such as signs, product displays, countertop dispensers, and shelf decorations to motivate sales. This kind of advertising serves two purposes. First, it is a reminder to customers that your product exists and that they need or want it. Secondly, point of purchase advertising can persuade a customer to buy one product over another. The way a product is displayed or merchandised can affect the buying decision.

Most point of purchase advertising is paid for by manufacturers. They send displays to the retailer along with the product hoping the retailer will use them in their store. Chances are the retailer carries several brands of the same product and it makes no difference to them which one they sell. Whichever sells best will receive more shelf space resulting in larger orders for the manufacturer.

Point of purchase displays gives manufacturers a means of reaching the consumer directly at the most crucial time in the buying process. Retailers also benefit from point of purchase advertising. Studies have shown that retailers who use point of purchase advertising generate more sales from the customers that visit their stores. In one study conducted by the Point of Purchase Advertising Institute, 56 percent of convenient store managers said that point of purchase materials are extremely effective in increasing sales. Forty-eight percent of supermarket managers also agreed.

Point of purchase advertising can be extravagant and expensive but it does not have to be. Guerrilla POP signs direct people to the things they came in to buy but they also steer customers toward other products they had not planned on buying. POP enlarges the size of transactions, stresses your selection and wins new customers as well as new profits. Think about what attracts you to certain products. Which bag of chips are you more likely to pick when you go to the corner convenience store, the one displayed on the neon-lit rack on the end of the aisle or the one stuffed in with all the other brands on the plain white metal shelf?

TARGETED MEDIA MARKETING

☞ **Your Gift Certificates**: Printing gift certificates is like printing money. Do not make the mistake of thinking gift certificates are solely the province of department stores. These days very juicy profits are being earned with gift certificates offered by movie theatres, massage therapists, computer stores, automobile dealers. This is an interesting one, automobile dealers give a gift certificate for parts and service. Book stores, shoe stores, ski areas, airlines and countless other types of businesses offer gift certificates.

Here is a little hint. Gift certificates work especially well for businesses that have never offered them before. People are always on the lookout for new and unusual gift ideas. Gift certificates often fit the bill perfectly. Hardware stores, video stores, and coffee bars are perfect places to offer gift certificates.

Start your program by printing a sign or adding a line to your brochure, insert, or ad that reads, "Ask about our gift certificates." A quality paper stock is recommended for the certificate printing. Make sure you include your business name at the top, leaving space for the dollar amount, and allow room for the name of the recipient. A testimonial about the value of your gift certificates will enhance your program. Make sure you do not have a cutoff date. Most people eventually use them, and despite the accounting hassle, telling a customer that the time has run out on their gift certificate is guaranteed to generate ill will and kill the sale.

As an alternative to the standard blank-check gift certificate try a more focused approach. Offer a gift certificate for a car wash every week for a year, or maybe a cup of espresso. By eliminating a cash value from the certificate you can make it even more attractive to the person giving the gift.

Most businesses today are going to gift cards. You see them everywhere. They are powerful, not only because they are gifts, but because people pack their card with your company name on it, in their wallet and they see it all the time. This is great repetition. You would also be surprised at how many regular customers you will have using gift cards for themselves. It saves the hassle of carrying cash.

Don't forget the most important opportunity. When you sell a gift certificate the profit to your business is not really generated from the first sale. A gift certificate is your opportunity to convert a first time customer into a repeat customer. Instruct your staff that gift certificate redeemers should be given extra special attention. This is your opportunity to dazzle them and make them regular customers. Most likely, they are first time customers so make sure you maintain a list of names and addresses of every customer who redeems a gift certificate in your store.

Follow up with a letter, a brochure, coupons, even a thank you note. You've just found someone who has already been given a testimonial from the person who gave them the gift certificate. Do everything you can to keep this new customer coming back as a paying customer.

☞ **Your Printed Brochures:** Promote with printed media. When somebody asks for information on your company, what do you send them? Many companies use out-of-date, incomplete, unfocused brochures that scare away more customers than they attract. Others use over-priced, over-produced extravaganzas that are just not effective enough to warrant their high cost.

Many businesses think of a brochure as an opportunity to close the sale without making the sales call. It is not the easy way out. Do not fall into this trap. For most purchases, that is expecting way too much. However, a brochure can do a great job of positioning your company and preparing the prospect to be sold.

Unlike an advertising insert, which you should spread far and wide, brochures should be distributed more selectively to those who have requested more information or to carefully targeted prospects because most purchasing decisions cause people some anxiety. They are afraid of making a mistake and reflexively hesitate before making a commitment.

More prospects will be converted if you ask them to take a few tiny steps rather than one giant leap. Most people will be more receptive to your invitation to buy if you ask them to take a small step, like reading the brochure. Then ask them to take another small step talk to you on the phone. Only after a couple of small steps do you ask them to take the step of buying something. This is also referred to as soft step marketing.

By adding these steps to the buying and the selling process, your brochure gives the prospect the opportunity to learn more about you. Customers must come to know and trust you before they commit to buying something and a brochure breaks the ice.

Let's talk about some advantages to using a brochure in the selling process. Number one, brochures work well when they amplify an introductory letter that initiates the relationship with the prospect. Brochures lend an aura of credibility to a company if they are professionally written, designed, and produced.

Brochures remove the pressure from the sale giving the prospect the chance to study what you have to say before you meet.

They enable you to answer important questions before the prospect even asks.

Use your brochure to give customers and prospects testimonials, to illustrate benefits, and to communicate verbally and visually. Many guerrillas skimp on their brochure design and production. That is a BIG mistake. Do not do it. This is your chance to position your company and establish a quality image.

Your brochure should be at least as well dressed as you are. That doesn't mean you have to have a 32-page four-color brochure at $5.00 a piece to compete with the big guys. There are two brochure types that have been successfully used by cost-cautious guerrillas. The first type is a three-fold brochure or a low-cost, full-color flyer folded into a booklet.

Nuts and Bolts for the Three-Fold Brochure

1. Make your cover headline stand out. People should know who you are without having to actually open your brochure. Your headline should sell your product and catch the reader's attention.

2. Include a graphic or photo on the cover that will draw the reader in. If possible, make it stand out with the use of color.

3. Include additional visuals throughout the brochure. Show your product or service in use.

4. Do not be afraid of long copy if it is needed. Give the prospect as much information as you can, describing clearly the benefits of your product or service.

5. Create a relationship with your prospect. Tell a little bit about yourself and your company. Share your business

credo, and establish the fact that you care about what you do and about your customers.

6. Include testimonials and a list of major clients or buyers that people can identify with.

7. Put useful reference material in your brochure that will make it worth hanging onto.

8. Let your prospects know how to reach you. Include your telephone number and address and web site at the very least. If you own a retail outlet, consider putting a local street map with your location starred on the brochure and include written directions.

9. Always include your hours of operation.

10. Ask for action. Include an order form, make an offer, or include a customer questionnaire in your brochure.

11. Always remember that color in a brochure adds to the professional quality. If you are going to use color, be sure to find a printer that specializes in color printing.

☞ **Your Video and Audio Brochures:** If anything can outdo a print brochure it is an electronic one, a five to nine minute version of a printed brochure. Video brochures combine the impact of a TV commercial with the targeted power of a mailed print brochure. The cost of duplicating short DVDs and CDs is approximately $1.50 - $2.00 each for one thousand or more.

The cost of producing videos is anywhere from $100.00 to $10,000.00 per minute, but you should anticipate that it will cost at least a thousand dollars a minute to really do a great job. You probably don't need more than four to five minutes for a final product, making the total cost of the video brochure only slightly more than a full-color print brochure. And, with a little computer savvy, you can make and edit your own, but be sure you can make it look really professional. A video brochure often gives a greater impression of worth and value than its printed equivalent.

Approximately eighty percent of Americans have access to a DVD or CD player making it possible to reach the majority of your audience with a DVD or CD. Prospects are likely to view it, and, if interested, will likely view it again with one or more people, in part because DVDs and CDs are still a novelty, unlike printed brochures. Most people do not instinctively throw them away.

Some large-scale Guerrillas have successfully executed mass mailings of video brochures. One car maker sent a video for a new model introducing the local dealer's name at the beginning, including glitzy footage in the middle and ended with the recipients name superimposed across the video image. It was the first of a series of personalized DVD brochures created by this Guerrilla and it was very effective.

Prospects can learn of your DVD through magazines, direct mailings, trade shows and other modes of communication. When they request a DVD or CD from you, send it to them for free. Include a personal letter just as you would with a printed brochure. Within ten days, follow up with a phone call or a letter. A request for a DVD should be construed as the first step in the purchasing process. Be sure to follow up. Do not lose the momentum you have created by failing to follow up.

Maybe you're not yet convinced about the power of video brochures. Read on: Camp Arrowan in Canada used to sell by word of mouth. They followed up every inquiry with a personal visit to the prospect's house. The closing rate for these visits was 10 percent. Unfortunately, this was time consuming and expensive. Two years ago they replaced the in-home visits with a video brochure. The closing rate has dropped slightly but the number of prospects has more then tripled. The camp is spending a lot less time and money to generate twice as many paying customers.

Creating an audio CD would be an alternative to a DVD. You save time and money with the audio version. The packaging of either should be a nice full color package introducing you and your company. Either one of these types, video or audio brochures, is very powerful.

☛ **Your Marketing Inserts:** Inserts take advantage of someone else's money. They offer a flexible, timely, and inexpensive means of reaching a highly targeted market. Find a marketer who has already reached the particular market you are interested in, insert your message along with theirs and you both win. Inserts can have a very low distribution cost. However, guerrillas know they must carefully manage the impact of any insert program by making sure it only goes to hot prospects.

As with any direct mail campaign, the quality of the prospect is much more important than the quantity. It does not do you any good to mail an insert to one hundred thousand people who have no use for, or interest in, your business. Do your research first.

Unlike brochures, inserts are never requested by the prospects so you have to overcome the clutter hurdle. Your insert must have impact. It must offer a benefit that is so irresistible it cannot be passed over. Use inserts to generate leads, to follow up with existing customers, to initiate or close a sale, and in support of a promotional campaign.

Several different types of advertising fall under the category of inserts. Package inserts are also called ride-alongs. These are direct mail pieces included in packages already being mailed to customers or prospects. Include them in your own mailings or contact a company that provides a related product. Arrange to include your insert in any of their mailings.

One guerrilla landscaper we know arranged to place a coupon for services in every statement sent out by the local gardening supply store. The landscaper reached his target market and generated new business. The gardening supply also won because the landscaper's clients always need to buy more gardening supplies and equipment. Those types of relationships really make sense.

What about free standing inserts? These are also called FSI's and are the tag along inserts that come in your daily newspaper. I am sure you've seen them. In fact, they probably drive you nuts. Most of the time they are produced by large companies aiming to blanket a huge market with coupons and word of a special sale. The advertiser pays to produce the insert and simply pays the newspaper to stuff it in the publication. The challenge with this is that it is not very targeted.

These types of campaigns can cost millions of dollars and they reach all sorts of people including those who have absolutely zero interest in your offering. So why am I telling you about it? Because, as a guerrilla, you can take advantage of this method and the technology behind it. Here's how. Your neighborhood paper probably isn't used to using FSI's. Offer to print a high quality, colorful insert they can stuff in their paper. If you have an ad salesman who is also a guerrilla, he will understand the importance of targeting a market. You might be able to have your insert included in the newspapers going only to certain zip codes.

Try testing your FSI by printing several different ones. Stuff them in regional editions of the publication and then track the response. This is a great approach for contractors, chiropractors, retailers, or anyone else targeting a specific neighborhood.

Let's talk for a moment about mailbox inserts. Every region of the country has a company that brokers direct mail inserts. You may even use one right now or perhaps you use several. Just look them up in the yellow pages if you don't. These brokers are in the business of collecting a number of local advertisers that want to share in the cost of sending an envelope filled with offers and coupons to every person in the neighborhood. These are your Valpacks, your Money Mailers, or your Advo's. These are prime examples of brand names used by brokers.

This is how they work. Brokers put together shared mailings by contacting a number of retailers in the same geographic area. You can contract a broker or you can do it yourself. Get together with several businesses in your neighborhood and send out a packet of inserts or coupons to all of your mailing lists. You will receive all the same benefits, but your mailing will be even more targeted. Many compatible businesses in the same neighborhoods do this, and they get excellent results.

And now, we'll talk about card decks. Not only are they magic for some guerrillas, but they are stacks of index cards that are mailed to targeted audiences, usually small businesses. Each deck contains 50 to 200 cards, each a tiny advertisement, usually with a business reply card on the back. The recipient flips through the deck stopping at anything that catches his eye. You've probably flipped through a stack you received in your own home mail. Because the decks are inexpensively produced, the cost of inclusion is low. It is possible to reach as many as one hundred thousand businesses for as little as $2,500. That's less than three cents a piece.

Decks are also highly targeted. Venture Communications, for example, brokers card decks such as the business and management card decks, the biochemistry and molecular biology card deck, and the teacher's card deck. As you can see, they can be very targeted.

Nuts and Bolts of Card Decks

1. A card deck's ability to target a niche is its greatest strength. Do your research and pick the deck that is right for you.

2. As with most types of advertising, the headline is the kicker. It has to be bold and meaningful. The person flipping through the deck has to be compelled to stop and read your card. If you can, take a look at the other cards in the card deck that are going out and make yours different. Make it a different color. Make it a different design. Make it stand out in any way possible. You may show a picture of your product. People rarely buy anything without seeing it. If possible, show the product in use.

3. Most importantly, the insert must call for action on the part of the prospect. Ask her to mail back the card order or to take advantage of a free offer. Give an 800 number or at least ask the prospect to fill out a questionnaire. If you do not ask for anything, you will not get anything. You get one chance with the card deck. If the prospect is not compelled to act on the spot, chances are your card will end up in the trash with everybody else's. So make it stand out. Call them to action.

4. Guerrillas rarely pay full price for card decks. Be sure to ask about remnant space or try to negotiate the price. Salespeople with these card decks are always willing to negotiate.

5. Look for card decks with repeat advertisers. If an advertiser buys space in a deck more than once, the ad is probably working for her.

6. Offer a free sample of your product or at least a free gift for ordering. It is the norm for card deck advertising and it is a great motivator.

Nuts and Bolts of Insert Ad Placement

1. Choose the right distribution program. It is very important to look for the demographics geared to your product or service. It is also important to try to ensure the merchandise your package insert accompanies will boost the response of your offer.

2. Test at least ten programs at a time. Out of every ten programs tested, you will have an average of three losers. That is normal. Experiment with new inserts to get an accurate measure of success.

3. Go with the maximum size. Different programs have different physical limitations, but always go with the maximum size allowed by each program to prevent your insert from being lost in the shuffle.

4. Test with copy that you know works. Do not write new copy, create new graphics, or introduce a new offer when you first test your insert. Test what you already know works in direct mail or spaced advertising. If your program fails, you will know it was the program and not your copy or offer that was at fault.

5. Be patient when evaluating a program. Inserts that accompany retail merchandise may take six months before they are fully distributed. Calculate a final cost per order you are comfortable with and as long as you come in under that number, consider your insert program a success.

6. Try to transform marginal performers into new profit makers. By reducing printing costs, changing layouts, changing stock, color, or copy, you might be able to manipulate the cost of the participation in a program. Creative renegotiation can turn a marginal program into a real success.

7. Include an appropriate number of inserts. When testing, you need at least 10,000 inserts in each program or your results may not be statistically reliable. On the other hand, if the number of inserts you put in one program is too high, it will force you to wait too long until all of your inserts have been distributed and you can evaluate the results. One way around this is to break up a large number of inserts into several keys and evaluate them as you go along. Always key every insert package using a five or six digit code as we have talked about. Mark every insert you send out with the key that will allow you to identify what package it was a part of. It is better to pay the extra to stop the press and change keys than it is to be unsure of your results.

8. Make sure you choose a dependable broker. Many inserts miss the program they are intended for because of foul ups in production or shipping. Your broker must make sure your materials are printed accurately, shipped to where they are supposed to go, received by the appropriate people, and inserted in the right program.

9. Always retest favorable returns. If you do not, a competitor may jump in and preempt you from profiting from your success. On the other hand, you should maintain sizable reserves of pre-keyed inserts so that you may take advantage of a new program or competitor's failure to retest properly.

Your Circulars or Flyers: For the money, circulars are one of the most powerful guerrilla-marketing weapons. They are pure power and pure economy. Why? 1) They get instant action. 2) They are astonishingly inexpensive (we're talking pennies here.) 3) They let you use color in a sea of black and white and, 4) They are the essences of simplicity and flexibility.

Circulars can be distributed in a variety of locations: posted on community bulletin boards, handed out on street corners, given to sports and music fans as they leave the game or the concert, placed on car windshields, included in your mailings, etc. You can even make deals with nearby non competitive businesses to place your circular in their stores.

Several years ago after the Arizona Diamondbacks won the World Series; they had a World Series parade in downtown Phoenix. We dressed up as strawberries and bananas and walked along with the parade, handing out circulars to people. This was a huge success and really increased our business over the next couple weeks. When you're creating a circular, one could save money by having a printer design and print the piece. With the explosion of desktop publishing and inexpensive copy-writing services it makes more sense to spend more of your money on a first-rate designer and writer and then photocopy whatever you need. Don't skimp on having the copy for your flyer well written. The difference between success and failure with a flyer often comes down to that detail.

Always remember the primary importance of an attention grabbing headline. Include your offer, its expiration date, your address, fax and phone number, and the major benefit or benefits you provide. While the bulk of the sales you generate through circulars will come soon after distribution, you want to establish a brand image for sales down the road.

With circulars, the biggest challenge is the effort it takes to get them well distributed. Consider hiring a high school student to distribute them door-to-door or on a busy street corner. Post them in your neighborhood on community bulletin boards, hand them out to people heading in to the local movie theater or the baseball park. Make a donation to your local church, and in return, ask them to stick a pile of your circulars on the tables during their next bake sale. Whatever you do, DO NOT hand them out in the middle of the mall or any other private establishment without first checking into the local laws regarding solicitation. All guerrillas play by the rules and play by the law.

Think before you act. Determine where your target market is likely to be. A Chinese restaurant places circulars under the windshield wipers of every car in the commuter parking lot. After all, every person parked there has a car, lives in the area, and will be reading the circular around dinner time, great targeting. A deli in Medford, Massachusetts, prints up two-sided circulars. One side offers a discount on a sandwich; the other side says "Go Jumbos." They hand out the circulars before Tufts University's football games and guess which circular gets held aloft every time the Tufts Jumbos score a touchdown? That's right.

Circulars are a great way to reach students. Make it humorous and you'll be practically guaranteed a response. Check your Yellow Pages under advertising circulars or distribution. Many cities have businesses that specialize in this service. Of course this is not as cheap as hiring a student, but it is more reliable.

☞ **Your Newsletter:** This is a great way to communicate with customers and prospects alike. The resourceful guerrilla looks for new and efficient ways to consistently remind the consumer of his name and business. One low-priced way to do this is with a newsletter. If your business becomes a source of information, as well as a source of products and services, you will gain respect and increased loyalty from all your customers.

A local fish market might use a newsletter to give customers recipes, tips on good values in fish, news about which fish are in season, etc. Who would ever think to do a newsletter at a local fish market? But it is effective. By positioning themselves as a company that really knows its fish, they gain credibility and help differentiate themselves from their competitors. According to Howard Penn Hudson, the president of the Newsletter Clearing House, newsletters are effective because they are targets, if you start a secretarial service, for example, you obviously want to reach business people.

Through the local Chamber of Commerce you can get a list of presidents of area businesses. Go directly to the decision makers who make the purchases. Send them a newsletter full of anecdotal stories from companies that use your service, citing benefits and testimonials. Make it easy for recipients to contact you for more information. Include a coupon or special offer with your newsletters. Do not be afraid to share your success.

If your business provides a service, send out an announcement whenever you sign a visible customer. Let everyone know which houses you are painting, which buildings you have rented, or how many hamburgers you have served.

If your newsletter is interesting enough, you can gradually turn it into a catalog and sell your prospects while you entertain them. Don't forget about co-marketing. Find several businesses that complement each other. For instance, maybe a plumber, an electrician and a painter. Combine their efforts into creating one newsletter that will help all three.

Nuts and Bolts of Designing and Writing a Newsletter

1. Fill your newsletter with interesting information, including short facts and blurbs that people find useful. If your newsletter is long or boring, you will lose your audience fast.

2. Proofread your newsletter carefully. It is a reflection of you and your company.

3. Be informative. Cover a variety of topics. Do not bore them by going on too long about any one thing.

4. Use your newsletter as a selling tool. Include your toll-free phone number, fax number and website, perhaps, on every page.

5. Be succinct. A newsletter does not have to be long to have impact. Most people look at a newsletter as something they can read quickly to get some useful information.

6. Invest in a designer for advice on layout and graphics. Once you have a professional design that works, stick with it.

7. Make your customer an important topic. People love to see their names in print.

8. Your newsletter is a selling tool, but it has to educate the reader too. Do not just fill it with advertising or you are going to turn off the reader.

9. Once you commit to a newsletter program, keep it coming regularly. Publish at least quarterly, but preferably bimonthly or even monthly.

10. Have specific goals in mind when you create your newsletter. It should have a voice and a focus. If you are confused about the purpose of your newsletter you can count on the fact that your audience will also be confused.

☞ **Your Reprints and Blowups**: If a newspaper or magazine runs a favorable story about your business, you can read it, do some back flips because of the free exposure, and let it fade from the public's memory or you can do several things to extend its lifespan. I would recommend the following:

Nuts and Bolts of Reprints and Blowups

1. Make reprints of the story and include it in your next mailing.

2. Make one large reprint of the story, frame it, and hang it in your store or reception area.

3. Include a reprint of the story as part of your next brochure.

4. Include excerpts from the story in your advertising campaign.

5. Mail the story along with the press release, fact sheet, and your photo, to a contact at a local radio or TV station.

6. Remember, news feeds upon itself, so make sure you leverage the power of reprints and blowups.

☞ **Your Posters**: Posters really pack a punch. Large, four-color posters that look more like art than advertising can be very effective marketing tools. Best of all, they are not as expensive as you might think. Once again, computers have come to the rescue. If you use traditional techniques to produce a four-color poster, the cost of color separation and printing are not cost-effective for short print runs. However, the whole process can be completely computerized. You can save hundreds of dollars if you only need a few dozen posters.

Nuts and Bolts of Using Posters

1. Posters make great in-store giveaway items. Customers, especially kids, love to get things for free.

2. Hang them around the store. The body shop uses huge ones to create a sense of excitement. They frequently change the posters, keeping their décor interesting to the customer. When the circus comes to town they hang posters all over the place. You can do the same thing to announce your special event. Cap, a videogame company, mailed a poster featuring their game graphics to the media on a monthly basis. If your poster is a piece of art, people will hold onto it and use it to decorate their room or an office, and your message becomes permanent.

3. Use your poster as a free-standing insert by inserting it into your local newspaper or regional magazine. Virtually every major town has at least one company that caters to graphic designers. They usually offer color copying, mounting, color rubdowns, and more. Check your Yellow Pages in the copying section, or look in the business to business directory under graphic designers.

☞ **Your Door Hangers:** If you run a geographically based business and want to let your prospective customers know about you, one of the best tools you can use is a door hanger. They are inexpensive to print and distribute, and they reach your prospective customers directly. A door hanger left at someone's house sends the message "I was here personally and I have something to say directly to you. As a customer, you are important to me." The most effective door hangers are the ones that look like oversized "Do Not Disturb" signs.

Success with this type of advertising depends heavily on, yet again, the right headline. Your door hanger must have an immediate impact on the recipient to produce results. A well-designed door hanger is sure to be read by the person who pulls it off the doorknob. As soon as the person picks it up, the message is conveyed. Now that is direct advertising.

The great thing about door hangers is that you are not competing with every other piece of mail because, usually, door hangers are delivered by themselves or in a situation called a "marriage" or a "ride along" where there are two or three door hangers. This way, it really gets the prospect's attention. The call to action should be primary: "You can eat a hot pizza tonight instead of cooking." Imagine the person coming home from a long day at work to find a door hanger with this headline and a coupon from the local pizzeria.

Nuts and Bolts of Door Hangers

1. A short, punchy headline is most effective

2. Don't skimp on the production. They are already inexpensive, so don't cut corners. Print your door hanger on a heavy paper or card stock and add a dash of color. Even make it full color when possible.

3. Use testimonials.

4. Describe your qualifications to provide the service. People need to know you are not just a fly-by-night operation.

5. Make an offer: a discount, a coupon, a free estimate or a free brochure – some type of call to action that induces the prospect to give you a call.

    Rarely does one marketing weapon do the entire selling job for a guerrilla.

But each one may get a guerrilla's foot in the door and that can lead to a prospect's name on an order form.

The ubiquitous restaurant menus that are indiscriminately dumped in apartment building lobbies in most cities are the worst kind of marketing. They do not have a catchy headline or special offer. Their approach is wasteful and annoying. You can be sure many restaurants have actually lost customers by invading prospects' home territory. Whenever you try a new advertising medium, make sure you do some research to ensure that you are not going to offend people.

It is easy to test door hangers, just code each one – either with a color or a little number on the bottom of the coupon – and track the results. Rotate offers within different neighborhoods. Also, be aware that this tactic can get tired. Most door hanger campaigns must be repeated several times before maximum results are realized. After all, a customer who does not order a pizza the first time he sees the offer may succumb the following week.

Check your Yellow Pages for door hanging companies in your area. Make sure you research the company, getting testimonials and referral letters from them to make sure that they are a reliable distribution company. Your other option is to hire a student or do it yourself.

In my Jamba Juice days, I used door hangers quite frequently and had a great amount of success with them. One store in particular had been in business for four years. We did a door hanging campaign offering people a free 16 ounce smoothie. Our cost on that was about 80 cents at the time. It was a very aggressive offer because we wanted to really grow that store.

We sent out 5,000 door hangers each week. We started the nucleus right at the store and the surrounding neighborhoods. We did 5,000 that week. The next week, we went out a little bit further, did another 5,000, the next week another 5,000, until we had distributed 20,000 door hangers. This was undoubtedly the best response I ever received on any marketing with Jamba Juice. We received a 15 percent redemption rate. Most direct mail pieces get 1 to 2 percent.

This store, already established four years, grew an average of fourteen percent for the following three years.

The first significant key to this was the aggressive offer. Second, we made sure we delivered on our product and our promise when they came in the store. Third, we had a great reliable company called Freedom Marketing that distributed the door hangers for us.

Your Catalog: Catalogs are a guerrilla tactic. They allow you to reach far more prospects, help position your company and your products, and make life easier for your customers. Your catalog does not have to look like the J Crew catalog to be effective. If the product or service you offer appeals to a select group of motivated people, even the simplest catalog can be incredibly effective. However, it really does help if your customer service and follow through is as good as J Crew's.

As a catalog marketer, you have to build your customer base one customer at a time. You can use your catalog as the primary salesperson, however, do not put out the catalog unless you are prepared to back it up with outstanding service and a lot of attentiveness to your customer's needs. There are three rules for catalog marketers.

1. Try a simple one or two page flyer first. Judge the response and then move on from there.

2. Target your mailings. The largest cost, by far, in catalogs is the cost of wasted mailings. Sending a catalog to someone who is not interested is like throwing money away. Start by sending the catalog to your existing customer list. Then expand by using carefully selected and researched mailing lists.

3. Test, test, test. As with many of the guerrilla marketing weapons, keep altering your lists, your catalog, your pricing, everything, until you have the mix that works for you.

Guerrilla catalog sellers take advantage of the mail order relationship to deal with each prospect on an individual basis. Because you are able to deal with each customer one on one, your business can start small and grow. Take advantage of every selling opportunity when producing your catalog. Obviously, the focus is on the products you are selling; their descriptions and their prices, but there are countless other ways to sell your products and your company.

Emphasize that your catalog is an extension of you. You are bringing your retail store to the customer, so take advantage of it. Make sure that you use all of the catalog's elements to make an impression on your customer and to sell your product. Make sure your catalog has a voice. There should be real people behind it. For example, the descriptions might read like personal recommendations.

Give the customer a visual frame of reference, so that he can characterize your company. This lends credibility to your company; something the customer needs before he buys from you. Welcome the customer just as you would if he walked into your retail store. Include a letter telling the customer how valuable he or she is. Sign the letter for a more personal touch.

Use your order form to its fullest potential to sell your product. Besides making the form easy to read, use, and understand, fill it with product descriptions and special offers. Select a product of the month from your catalog and pre-print the product number and price on the order form. Then, all the customer has to do to order the item is check the box next to it. And as everything else, make sure that you include testimonials throughout the catalog.

Written letters of recommendation from customers who have already purchased your products will definitely boost credibility. When prospects see that others have benefited, they will want to order too. Besides, if they order, they become part of your club. Remember that according to a survey, 36 percent of people shop by mail because it is convenient. Make it even more convenient to shop in your catalog and you will gain the edge over your competition very fast.

Make sure you guarantee satisfaction. While there is no way to guarantee the customers will actually get what they expect, the next best thing is to promise that you will take the merchandise back if the customer is not completely satisfied.

Also, the copy of your catalog has to be consistent and reflect the character of the products being sold. Your catalog can be snobbish, loud, educational or folksy in nature, regardless of the particular message you want to convey, its copy must be clear, concise and contain all the basic information.

Nuts and Bolts of Creating Catalog Copy

1. Keep your copy straightforward and concise. You want to give the reader as much information as possible in as clear a manner as possible.

2. Motivate the prospect to buy. Get them excited about your product. Your catalog is your salesperson so give it your very best pitch.

3. Make sure the photograph or illustration matches the copy.

4. Compliment the reader with your copy. Only "you" are worthy to own this type of shirt.

5. Make your copy timely in nature. If your catalog is scheduled to come out during the Christmas season for example, make a lot of references to Old St. Nick.

6. Make your order form simple and easy to understand, but detailed enough that the customer will not have any problems following directions.

7. Highlight the key selling points of each item and repeat them at least twice.

8. Make your headlines sing out. They have to make the browser stop and look. The copy should convey the identity of not only the product, but of your company as well. All the elements of your catalog need to come together to form an image to which the customer can relate.

Some final guidelines for catalog marketing: Set specific objectives on what the catalog should do for your business. Define your audience so that you know who will be receiving your catalog. This helps in creating and producing it. Make sure you preplan all the elements of your catalog business before going into production that includes product, prices, fulfillment, and more. If possible, organize your offering into clearly defined groups so that the catalog is not all hodgepodge.

Make a rough outline of the contents of your catalog, including everything you wish to have in it. The order form, promotional inserts, products, etc. Make sure that you determine the exact format you want, size, typeface, color or no color, type of paper, the binding. Make a layout that is organized, logical and pleasing to the eye of your target audience. And finally, plan right and perfect the copy. Then set up a timetable and stick to it.

Your Online Marketing: There is a lot to know about online marketing. We will only cover it briefly here, pointing out the most important parts. If you want to learn more about it, I highly recommend the book "Guerrilla Marketing Online" by Jay Conrad Levinson and Charles Ruben. There are several editions each worth the investment.

There are six avenues of marketing online:

1. Send email to people who want to receive it. Many do. Remember, guerrillas do not engage in junk emailing, known as spamming. Guerrillas do, however, have software called auto responders which enables them to automatically send email to people who request it. Get people on your email list to send weekly or monthly letters, industry information, etc. This is a great way to stay in touch with your prospects. One very important word of caution – do not send daily emails. People will get tired of you fast because they are busy. Make sure the information you send is not an advertisement but real, useful, information.

2. The second online avenue is chat sessions for those who are interested in the topic of your business. You can get feedback, prove your authority and credibility and most

importantly establish relationships with people around the world or within your community.

3. Participate in online forums and newsgroups where you can post messages. Respond to questions, without being too pushy. Herald your company as a source of excellent products and information.

4. Post classified ads in the many sections in which you can do so at no cost or low cost. You might combine audio and video with your online verbiage. If you choose this avenue, post your ad daily. The newest ads appear at the tops of the listings.

5. The fifth avenue of online marketing is to write articles. Articles are published on many online services. Prove your expertise and include your phone number and email address. The more you give away online, the more you will get.

6. Host conferences using online services. Here, you get into interactive conversations with large groups of people, all of whom attend the conferences to hear what you have to say. We do this with the weekly Wednesday Guerrilla Marketing calls for members of the Guerrilla Marketing Association. By the way, if you are not a member yet, you can become one by going to our website, www.gmarketingstrategies.com. I highly recommend it.

☞ **Your Direct Mail:** One of the most powerful marketing weapons available is direct mail. It is targeted, easy to test and generally low cost. It allows you to contact prospects directly, make your pitch, and invite them to become customers. Big budgets have no advantage inside the mailbox. Unlike direct mail giants like LL Bean, your goal is not to stuff a catalog into every mailbox in America. Instead, by focusing your energy and your dollars on a very small, highly targeted population, you can translate postage into big dollars. Direct mail allows a David to compete with a Goliath. It is the great equalizer.

The good news for guerrillas is that very often non-guerrillas don't have the patience to attract one customer at a time. While large companies worry about market segments and media plans you can focus on who lives in suburban Illinois. The entire key to direct mail success revolves around testing. You must constantly test and evaluate both the successes and the failures. Send out two different offers and monitor which offer gets the most response. Try different pricing scales or different order forms. Direct mail is the best way to study your market. Be patient with testing and make sure that you do it.

The advantages of direct mail over other advertising media include, 1) You can measure results more accurately. It is so important to measure your results. With direct mail you can do that. 2) You can be as expansive or as concise as you would like. You can really zero in on almost any target audience. You can personalize your marketing which has such great impact. 3) You have unlimited opportunities for testing. You can develop repeat sales to proven customers and you can compete with and even beat the giants.

Three key elements to consider when using direct mail are the list, the offer, and the package. Of the three, can you guess which one is the most important? Did you guess the list? The list is by far the most important. Choosing the right list is the crucial difference between success and failure in direct mail. Most people do not realize just how scientific and targeted the list business has become. For a cost of less than $0.10 a name you can buy mailing labels for members of an unbelievable number of groups. List rentals are a major source of income from many publications and direct mailers. By offering their list to other marketers at a cost ranging from $50.00 to $100.00 per thousand, list managers are able to generate substantial income. As the market clamors for more specialized lists the managers respond.

Here are some examples: What about doctors who have purchased medical stat kits by mail? Yes, you can find them. What about subscribers to the Zi News who live in downtown Chicago? Absolutely. You can find a list for almost any type of person or demographic in the United States. Do not forget to start with your own customer list. It is the most effective list you can use because your best sales prospects are your existing customers. Then use rented lists to expand your market.

You need to focus like a laser. Non-guerrillas are pre-occupied with volume and buy names by the millions. They do not use the specialized lists that are ideal for the guerrilla who knows that mailing to 100 people who have an interest in their product is much more effective than mailing to 1,000 unqualified leads. You get much better response from mailing to 100 people who have an interest in your product than 1,000 unqualified leads. Most people do not understand that concept.

Your first step is to browse the SRDS, the Standard Rate and Data Service. This massive book contains more than 10,000 different mailing lists. There are also companies out there you can find on the Web. These lists allow you to carefully select exactly which group of people you will be marketing to. If you can define the precise market you are selling to, and you ought to be able to do that in your sleep, you can find a mailing list that is ideal for you and your product.

There are subscribers to magazines, members of clubs, purchasers of similar products, demographic groups and more. In addition to these commercially available lists guerrillas often barter their own customer lists for less well known but often more effective lists. A carpenter could trade his customer list with a plumber, or travel agent might buy a list of soon to be married couples from a cater-er. Even if there are only 50 names on a mailing list it can turn into a significant asset. When you rent a list you are usually granted only one use. However if the person you mail to responds to you then you own that name.

As you rent and use the lists, keep careful records of how each list performs and segregate the people who respond from those who do not. Lists get stale quickly because as many as 20 percent of the people on the list move every year. Make sure your list is as up to date as possible. Once you find a list that works for you, be sure you periodically contact the list manager for the latest addi-tions to that list. This new flow of names is virtually guaranteed to do as well as the last batch. Too many guerrillas focus on the cre-ative aspect of the package without worrying about the list. The list is king.

The Direct Mail Offer: Every direct mail piece invites the recipient to take action even if it is only to call for a free estimate or a free sample. The goal is to offer the prospect something so irresistible he or she will immediately order it.

Some people test the creativity of their direct mail piece and fail to spend enough time on the offer. Many will test the color of the paper, the size of the package, and the use of a photo versus a drawing, etc. This is actually the simplest part of the three elements in your direct mail package. If your offer is not effective you are guaranteed to fail. Make sure that you have a powerful offer.

Janet Hughes and Associates Marketing Consultants wage a very effective direct mail campaign. Every month they mail out a piece to prospects and existing customers that highlights a different aspect of the service that Janet Hughes provides. On one mailer the prospect is asked to fill out and fax back a brief questionnaire. They have been running the campaign for over two years and receive an average of 25 calls per quarter in response. Eleven or twelve of those inquiries usually turn into paying clients for the firm.

Some special offer alternatives you might consider are:

1. A 30 day free trial.

2. A free gift with a purchase.

3. Allow installment payments.

4. You might sell your product for a higher than retail price.

5. Sell your product for a lower than retail price.

6. You may offer to send your product by COD.

7. Give people the choice of being billed later.

8. Offer a free gift for allowing you to set up a demonstration. Whatever it is, make your offer excellent!

The most celebrated part of direct mail selling is creating the package. This begins with the stamps and appearance of the mailing package you use and includes the paper, the copy, the layout, and the design of the piece itself. While your list and your offer are far more important than the creative element, this is the part you can haggle over forever.

If you are doing a large scale direct mailing to a broad audience you may want to use an envelope teaser to grab their attention. After all, if your envelope is not opened it doesn't matter how wonderful your package is. Here are some ideas that will help you create even better material. Envelope teasers are a great way to get people to look inside. Some envelope teaser ideas include:

1. Free gift enclosed!

2. Money saving offer inside!

3. Wealth building secrets for the new millennium!

4. Private information for your eyes only!

5. Did you know that you can double your profits?!

6. What every business like yours needs to know!

7. How to add new profits for only $0.06 a day!

8. See inside for exciting details about _____!

9. Read what's in store for you this week only!

There are a lot of different things you can use just make it creative while remembering that your goal is to get your envelope opened.

Of course, getting the envelope opened it just the beginning. Getting a response is the next important step. Let's talk for a few moments about how to get a 22 percent response rate.

My favorite campaign of all time involved a target market of 1,000 to whom a company was trying to sell an expensive product. In order for the project to succeed the company needed to receive at least a 10 percent response rate on the mailing. They started by using Federal Express to deliver the letters. While using FedEx in small quantities can be very expensive, they are happy to negotiate a special rate for anyone willing to mail 1,000 letters in one day. Use your bargaining techniques with FedEx.

In this case, the company was able to negotiate with FedEx to deliver the letters for approximately $6.00 per letter. Inside, the recipient found a laser printed letter mail merged to include their name, address and firm. Their name and the name of their firm was mentioned several times in the letter. There was also a handwritten post-it note on the letter. Every package was followed up with a personal phone call. Nearly 100 percent of the respondents opened the letter. More than 50 percent took the salesman's follow-up call. And, an incredible 22 percent of the respondents, which is 220 people, ordered the product sending in a check for how much? $1,000.00. As you can see, the cost of the mailing was tiny compared to the amount of revenue it generated.

If you sell a product or service that is very attractive to a small group of people, consider testing a similar campaign.

Nuts and Bolts for Direct Mail Marketing

1. The most important element is the right list.

2. Make it easy for the recipient to take action.

3. Letters almost always do better in packages than without.

4. The best buyers are those who have bought by mail before.

5. Do anything to get your envelope opened. Unopened mail is another word for "trash."

6. Keeping good records is absolutely paramount.

7. Testimonials improve the response rate.

8. Remember that nothing is as simple as it seems and it does take work. It does take creativity and thought.

Including a business reply card in your mailing is a good way to encourage response. Sometimes people will not respond to a direct mail piece because it is too much work for them either to call you on the phone or to stuff something into an envelope, address it, and mail it. However, if it is easy, if all they have to do is respond by checking off a box on your reply card and stick it in the mail, they are more likely to do so. Here's the catch with simplifying what people need to do to respond; if you make it too easy you may get a lot of responders who are not really serious about buying your product. You will have to spend a lot of time weeding them out as you follow up on your mailing. Still, a business reply card is effective. If you want to set up a business reply account call your local post office.

Nuts and Bolts for Improving Your Business Reply Card (BRC)

1. State the offer clearly.

2. Avoid writing like a lawyer. Make your copy sound like it was written by an accessible human being.

3. Write with energy and personality.

4. Stress that the offer is risk free. People do not want risk.

5. Include check boxes. If there are ordering options, check boxes are a must. If there are no options put a pre-checked box in front of the "yes."

6. Make your 800 number stand out and easy to see.

7. Put important information on the front.

8. Use visuals to spur action and guide the reader.

9. Make sure that you attach a stub. BRCs often get better results when there is a stub perforated along the edge of the card. What should go back there? How about a copy of a money back guarantee that the buyer can retain for his or her own records?

10. Give your business reply card an appropriate title. Instead of calling your BRC an "order form" or "order card" try "action card" or "preferred customer upgrade card."

We have talked about testing a lot but I must reemphasize it. When sending direct mail a guerrilla always tests. No one knows why one direct mail works better than another but, unlike most things in this world, it is easy to tell. Either your direct mail letter works or it does not. We know that long letters do better than short ones, that letters received on Tuesday do the best and that adding a PS always increases response. None of these facts necessarily makes any sense at all. The only way they were discovered was by testing them.

Every mailing should contain at least one test. Larger mailings should contain more than one. While the need for testing seems obvious, many smaller direct mail marketers do not test as often as they should. The following example points out how important testing can actually be.

If you mail 100,000 letters with a 2 percent response rate you will receive 2,000 orders. If you can increase the rate to 2.1 percent you will get 100 more orders. If your profit-per-order is $100.00, that equates to $10,000.00.

Test your copy, the size of the envelope, the type of stamp, the color of the ink, the type style you use, the photos, ...test everything!

Nuts and Bolts of Testing

1. Run tests on a random distribution of the same list. Do not test one mailing in Denver and the other in Reno. It simply will not work.

2. Test only one thing at a time. If you change copy and color at the same time you will never know which one actually made the difference.

3. Test on at least 200 names at a time. You probably do not need to test on more than 400. Statistically, that is more than necessary.

Keep track of your tests by putting a little three digit code on the bottom of your coupon. In fact, make sure the code is on something the recipient will have in her hand when she calls your 800 number to order. Instruct your operators to ask for the code. It will make it easy for you to figure out which calls came from where.

More Nuts and Bolts of Testing - Elements to Consider when Testing

1. Color versus black and white printing.

2. Motivators.

3. Pricing of your product.

4. Length of the letter.

5. First class versus third class delivery.

6. Your mailing list.

7. Your envelope color and treatment.

8. Your means of ordering.

9. The number of enclosures in your envelope.

10. Postage paid versus buyer pays. Return postage versus toll free numbers.

11. One step versus two step conversion.

12. How do you ask people to buy from you? Do you ask them to respond immediately? Do you ask them to call and receive a brochure? Or do you ask them to set up a meeting and then ask them to buy from you?

☞ **Your Direct Mail Postcard:** In the direct mail category, post cards are considered a little bit different. If you are about to do a direct mailing you might try it with a postcard because you can save money and increase your response rate at the same time. Make it a colored postcard and you will get the best of both worlds. Color actually increases readership by 41 percent and raises a buyer's inclination to buy by 26 percent. The cost? It is lower than you think.

Direct mail can be expensive at a cost of nearly $1.00 a letter by the time you include postage, envelope, inserts, stuffing and handling. At a response rate of one or two percent you can see why you need a hefty profit per order to make it actually worth your while. Direct mail postcards are less expensive. You are saving about a dime per piece in postage. You do not have an insert or an envelope and you do not have to stuff. I figure you can get a postcard mailing out the door for less than about $.40 each. Ask your local postmaster before printing your postcards how much it will cost to send them. There are certain size limits you should also be aware of.

Postcards are also successful because people do not have to open the postcard. The chance that they will at least glance at the message is much greater. Postcards are lousy at closing a sale but very good at making announcements or getting someone's attention.

When you design your postcard remember that you get only one chance to make that impression. As always, make sure your headline is dynamic. Use colored paper or two color printing, black and red ink for example. If you can, test a full-color postcard with a photo of your product on it because your prospect's first impression is so important. Pay special attention to the colors that you test. The right colors may double your sales.

The maximize size for a $.23 postcard is 4¼" by 6". Do not be afraid to turn your postcard sideways and design it so it is 6" wide by 4¼" inches tall. Be creative with it and use the postcard in the ways it fits your product.

Nuts and Bolts of a Direct-Mail Postcard Campaign

1. Announce a private sale to your best customers

2. Announce the grand opening of a new store to your best customers.

3. Offer a secret sale discount or a special contest.

a. Bring this card with you to be entered into our special drawing.

4. Share a good review. This is great for restaurants or theaters.

5. Announce the promotion or a new hire. This is great for hairdressers. There are a lot of different ways you can use direct-mail postcards. Just make sure that you follow all the guidelines.

Your Database Marketing: Database marketing is the perfect weapon for any guerrilla, big or small. It gives you a way to dominate your competition by using your knowledge of your customers to deliver unique products and services. Now, with the power of computers, you can divide and recombine your customer list in a thousand ways depending on your knowledge of every single customer. Today your customer list can help you create new niches to expand and deliver new products to.

Take a new look at your customer base. Think of every customer as an individual, not as a mass-market statistic. Database marketers make the extra effort to learn about their customer's individual interests, needs, and desires. They create relationships based on what they have learned and market to those same individuals over and over and over again. For example, if you had a list of every customer who bought fax paper last month you could contact them again this month to arrange for a refill order. If you know what your customers want even before they do, you can provide it for them before your competitors can.

Technology has opened the doors to database marketing for small businesses of all kinds. It is the great equalizer and it can, in fact, help you not only compete with the big guys but surpass them in the marketplace. Ironically, it is the technology that allows you to reach your customers on a very personal level.

Your mailing list is maintained on a computer database, right? If not, it should be. Take great pains to keep that database of customers and prospects current. Every time you learn something about a customer put it in your database. If you knew which 250 of your customers were most likely to buy extra large Christmas trees you could send them a letter two weeks before your shipment arrived, thereby guaranteeing that they would find the tree that they want, and that they will buy it from you, not your competitors.

Each time a Guerrilla sells something to a new customer she realizes the value that customer could have to her business over the long haul. She does not just sell the product and call it quits. She records what the customer purchased, when and why she purchased it, and when she may need to make a repeat or related purchase. Remember the Guerrilla keeps that information in her computer database and sends out a friendly reminder or a coupon when she gets a special shipment of an appropriate product or when the computer tells her it is time for the customer to buy again.

There is a lot of power in database marketing. Make sure you keep your database current and use it to market to your current customers over and over again.

☞ **Your Customer Mailing List:** Customer lists are the goldmine of an established business. Remember this, keeping an existing customer and increasing your business with him is far, far easier than finding a new customer. Yet, very few businesses spend enough time selling to their existing customer base. Start your customer mailing list on the day that you open and never, never stop collecting names.

Nuts and Bolts of Generating Mailing Lists

1. Whenever you deal with someone who calls your business, take his or her phone number right at the start. If you offer to send the person a brochure or free coupon, you have her address too.

2. When a customer leaves something, shoes for repair or dry cleaning or special order, make sure you get their address and phone number.

3. Run frequent sweepstakes that require customers to fill out a form with their name, address, and phone number. For example, the owners of a new hockey team in Norfolk, Virginia, went to every business to business trade show they could find when they first moved into the area. At each show they placed a fishbowl at their table and invited people to toss their business cards in the bowl for a free chance at winning a hockey jersey. The contest generated traffic at the table and also provided the owners of the team with an immediate list of names and addresses of people to whom they sent tickets and advertising sales material. Several people who entered that contest eventually became some of the teams' most loyal fans and corporate sponsors.

4. Install a prominent suggestions box. This is not only good business, it also gives you a way to collect addresses, email addresses, phone numbers, etc. Not only should you place the names of people who enter suggestions on your mailing lists, you should also respond personally to each suggestion. Send a hand written note to the person thanking him for his input; a great first step in trying to build your business one customer at a time.

5. Create a free newsletter catalog and offer it to anyone who gives you their name, address, or phone number. Insert an offer with your product that requires customers to write in to redeem it. For example, Mr. Coffee prints an offer on the inside of their coffee filter packages for one of their water purifiers. Not only are they reaching hot prospects for another one of their products, but they are also collecting names and addresses for their database. Customers must fill out and mail in the form to take advantage of the water purifier offer.

6. All products sold in this country come with an automatic implied warranty. Smart marketers insert a warranty card. Even though there is little legal basis for the card, the warranty stands whether you mail it in or not. It is also a great tool to find out more information about your customers. The warranty card collects names and addresses as well as other valuable marketing information.

7. Offer a new customer starter kit that includes coupons, a catalog, and other things.

8. Put a fishbowl on your counter and invite your customers to throw their business cards in to win something from your store. For example, if you own a shoe store, tell people to drop their names and addresses in the bowl and after they buy five pairs of shoes you will give them the sixth for free. An important key to this is to make sure you state on the fishbowl or the box in which you are collecting addresses, that you are going to put them on your mailing list. That way you can make sure you do not offend anybody or run into spamming problems. This is one way to get the customer's consent before putting them on your list.

Now that you have the names what are you going to do with these mailing lists? Well here are some ideas. Send a coupon good for 10 percent off any purchase. Highlight different areas of your store and be sure to attach an expiration date to get people to visit you now. Send greeting cards on holidays, birthdays etc. Send key chains, pocket knifes, pocket flashlights, little plastic pumpkins. Send something once a month. Clip articles and send them to customers who might be interested. Send a thank you note after any particularly big purchase. It furthers your relationship with a customer at a critical moment. Start a company newsletter featuring a variety of topics, including car care tips, high school sports news, neighborhood news, new product news especially good for hobbies etc. Even press clippings and achievements.

Another thing you can use your mailing list for is to send magazine subscriptions; great for dentists, barbers, even floor waxing and chimney cleaning companies. They have a high perceived value and remind your customers of you regularly. Get creative with these lists. They are powerful. Once you have a customer, make sure you continue to market to them regularly. They are your greatest source of income.

☞ **Your Order Form:** The seemingly small detail of the inclusion and the design of an order form is actually very important. If you sell by direct response or with a catalog, your order form may be the last hurdle between the customer and the order. First, your order form should be as user friendly as possible. It should include your guarantee, easy ordering instructions, and even new or special product highlights or promotions. Introduce new products.

When you introduce a new product, highlight it on the order form. Your regular customers might not realize that you have something new and they will appreciate the chance just to check it out. If you want to offer a free trial, this is a great place to mention it.

Highlight special deals and promotions. When you print your order forms, consider writing the special deals along the side by hand. This personal touch will attract attention and personalize your presentation at the critical deciding moment.

As a test, sit down with your form and time how long it takes to fill it out. Are there sections that are confusing? Are you asking the customer to do work that you could be doing, computing tax, figuring freight, etc. You need to make it very user friendly.

Shortsighted policies can cripple even the best conceived Guerrilla Marketing efforts. Hanna Anderson, usually a Guerrilla, presents its wares in a beautiful, order-friendly catalog. But when the user confronts the order form, he sees shipping charges that can account for as much as 25 percent of the order total. By making it hard to do business, Hanna Anderson may be turning away some potential customers.

Offering different ordering and payment methods makes it easier for people to do business with you. For repeat customers, offer automatic debiting, credit card payment, or subscription rates, even if they are not normally associated with your business. You would be surprised at how many people find paying the bills, especially small ones, a big hassle. Many mortgage banks have discovered this and greatly increase profitability and cash flow by offering to deduct payment directly from their bank account.

If you run a local newspaper, try allowing your customers to pay by credit card, rather than always requiring a check. Another thing to consider is this: You would be surprised by how many people fill out your form, but you never see it because it never gets mailed. Allow people to fax you their orders. Or, if you want them to use the mail, include a business replay envelope in your catalog. You should always do everything you can to make the order process easy and flexible.

TRADITIONAL MEDIA MARKETING

☞ **Your Yellow Page Ads**: Imagine a publication that went to every household in your market for free and it was used extensively only by people who were serious about buying a product or service every time they used it. Would you be interested in this advertising? It is the Yellow Pages. Too often, because of their cost, the Yellow Pages are under-used by many Guerrillas. However, there are also thousands of businesses that attributed their entire success to Yellow Pages advertising and clever Guerrillas can and should use this effective, though expensive medium to their advantage.

Unlike other media, Yellow Pages ads are difficult to test because they only run once a year and they are plagued by countless rules enforced by the publisher of the directory. Your Yellow Pages sales rep is the fountain of knowledge but he is also trying to sell you the biggest possible ad. Press him for whatever information you can but be sure to make your own decision about what you and your business can afford.

Nuts and Bolts of Yellow Pages Ads

1. The copy. Include as much copy in the Yellow Pages advertisement as you can possibly fit. Studies have shown that display ads with more information stimulate customer action. Russell Marketing Research conducted

a study where a set of prospective respondents were shown ads that were both heavy and light in terms of the amount of copy. The study revealed that the heavy copy ads drew more response by an average ratio of more then two to one. It has been repeatedly shown that more copy sells. The more information you can convey to the prospective buyer the better.

2. The size. Make your ad as large as possible within the constraints of your budget. In the same study cited above, respondents claim that they would call the advertiser with the largest ad first by an overwhelming percentage. The larger the ad the more information you can convey and the more persuasive you can be. If prospects ignore your ad it does not matter what you say. Color is also an important factor. If possible, include a second color in your ad because color attracts readers. Convince the prospective buyer that you are reliable. Include information along the lines of the following: years in business, experience, size of firm, licenses, certifications, degrees, awards. If you are the largest pizza parlor in town, say so. State the brand names, trademarks, manufacturers and dealers with whom you do business. Include any information about distribution and factory service depots. Mention any insurance, bonding, guarantees, association memberships and specially trained employees. Convince the prospective buyer that you are the best and the most complete dealer for the product or service. Include types, scope, variety, cost, and quality of service or product. Do not forget to mention specialized services and features, availability, inventory, capacity, catalogs or brochures, financing, credit cards

accepted, check cashing, pickup and delivery, hours and parking. As you can see, we recommend packing everything you can into your ad. Pictures and illustrations are interesting to look at and also help to attract the prospective buyer's eye. They can also help tell the story of your product or service. Consider inserting a picture of the owner, premises or product. It is also a great idea to include your company name and logo in very big type and most importantly, include your location. Let people know where they can find you. Include your nearest intersection, landmarks, shopping center, or, if necessary, even a little map.

You can get a big bang for your buck with Yellow Pages advertising if you follow those simple tips for effective Yellow Page ads.

Your Article Writing: Remember, people buy from people they trust. They want to know that you are an authority in your field before they spend their money with you, especially if you are in a service profession. As mentioned in the public relations weapon, editors of newspapers and magazines are hungry for information to write about. Give them that information. Start with the really localized newspapers and magazines. They will be the easiest to get into. Then you use them as samples to give to larger regional magazines and newspapers. One rule of thumb: give information only. Do not try to sell anything or you will lose your credibility.

Part of becoming an authority is not being sales-y. This is so important I will repeat it this way: Do NOT sell in any way, shape, or form when writing an information article. You will, of course, have your contact information at the bottom. After you have written an article or two and those articles have been published, use them in your marketing. Put a copy up on your website, a copy in your office or your store. You can even use them in your direct mail pieces. You will be surprised at the credibility you achieve with writing articles.

☞ **Your Column for Publication:** Writing a column is even more powerful than one hit articles. All of the same rules and guidelines for writing articles applies to writing a column. Start with articles to build your credibility and gain samples to get the publication to run the column. Columns are generally weekly or monthly. Again, start with the localized newspapers and magazines. Also, and very important, never, ever think about charging a fee for your column. You are going for fame, not fortune on this one and believe me, you will get it.

☞ **Your Classified Ads:** Classified ads reap dynamic results running them in newspapers, magazines, and newsletters. The greatest strength of classified ads is their ability to reach honest prospects. Most people reading any particular portion of the classified section are seriously interested in buying something.

Classified ads reach prospects with such accuracy that they often outpoll display ads costing much, much more. This is true since the classified ads have targeted sections such as antiques, travel, computer equipment and so forth.

Classified ads can be part of an expensive but highly profitable mail order campaign if you take advantage of the high circulation of some of the national newspapers and magazines with classified sections.

☞ **Your Newspaper Ads:** Newspapers range from national to metropolitan to neighborhood, from campus to ethnic to trade, from classified to shopper to business, and from daily to weekly to monthly. All should be considered.

The greatest strength of newspapers is news so make sure that you present your information in a newsy manner to capitalize on the mindset of that reader. Look into the different zones of newspaper distribution. Many newspapers have zones which will make it easier for you to target your marketing. Without zone editions, newspaper is generally too expensive for the average business to use effectively.

If a person advertises in the San Fransico Chronicle, with an ad two columns wide by five inches tall, they would pay about $1,000.00 and the ad would be seen by many who are too far away from the business to even consider going there. On the other hand, using one of the five zones the Chronicle offers, a business can target the zone surrounding their business costing about $120.00 for the same ad.

With newspaper advertising, remember that, generally, it is more effective to run six small ads in the same issue or spread over a few issues than it is to run one big ad. This goes back to the repetition principle. As with all marketing, make sure you test a few different types of ads along with different sizes.

Your Magazine Ads: Magazine ads can be just as powerful as newspaper ads. There are two categories of magazines for you to consider: consumer magazines and trade magazines. Of the consumer magazines, some are national and some are local. The greatest strength of all magazines is reader involvement.

Another major advantage offered by magazines, perhaps more than any other medium, is credibility. The credibility the readers attach to the magazines is unconsciously bestowed upon you. Anyone who thinks they can't buy credibility might consider ads in prestigious magazines aimed at their prospects.

Another reason to check into magazines as a potential marketing weapon is for their powerful reprint value. You can run a full page ad in 2005 and continue to mail reprints in the year 2089. Each reprint would say as advertised in *Time* magazine or whatever publication you selected. This is powerful. People trust most magazines so they will trust you and your company.

Magazines also help you clearly target your audience. We have a doctor client that just opened a laser and skin clinic in San Antonio. We suggested *The San Antonio Woman* for their target audience. You can target even more specifically many categories such as prospects interested in photography, cooking, skiing, home decorating, gardening, etc.

☛ **Your Radio Commercials:** Radio advertising is one of the most powerful guerrilla tools available. Radio stations are receptive to remnant and barter deals and they usually need what you have to offer. Play your cards right and you can receive three times more radio exposure than you pay for.

Some of the benefits and keys to successful radio advertising are that radio is one of the best ways to reach highly targeted markets. To do this however, you have to make sure you are advertising on the right station. Do your research to pinpoint the stations in your market whose listeners most closely resemble your customer base.

Radio works best in combination with other media, just like many other marketing tools. Use it to reinforce a direct mail or telemarketing campaign. It also works well in conjunction with 800 or 900 telephone numbers. Be creative in your radio advertising. A humorous approach gets attention. Radio provides a great bang for the buck. Short commercials are great for building name recognition and long commercials give you plenty of time to tell your story, but don't fill the time with dead space or boring copy. Sixty seconds is an eternity on the radio.

Remember the principle of repetition. It is even more important on the radio than anywhere else because listeners tune in and out, do errands, drive through tunnels, and occasionally stop paying attention. You need to repeat yourself several times.

Use the radio's live power. Have the station do a live remote from your place of business. The disc jockey drives a huge van to your parking lot and does his broadcast live. This is a particularly effective campaign if you're promoting a special event like a grand opening or a sale. Live remotes are a call to action. Come right down and whatever you're going to say. Remotes also get you far more ads for less money than the conventional radio campaign ever could. The station wants to draw attention to remote broadcasts and to you, and remotes are great for advertisers because they also allow the radio station to show off. Who doesn't like to show off, right?

Radio is a powerful medium. You can create the sense of urgency that just doesn't happen in print. Combine efforts with other businesses or organizations to create an attention-getting promotion. Hold a food drive at your place of business for a local charity. Advertise on the radio and use a live remote to push the drive. Run a contest asking for entries in your radio commercials. Institute a new toll-free number service line and plug it on the radio.

Radio is a particularly effective medium for car dealers. What better time to run an ad about jeeps than during rush hour in a snowstorm.

Radio is the ultimate remnant space medium. Offer to pay the station for any unsold time during the day. Whenever the station has a couple of unsold minutes, they will run your ad for a small fee. You get low-cost exposure and the station gets a little something for time that would have gone unsold.

Remember, radio stations are often open to bartering. If you own a restaurant, offer to provide free lunch for the DJs on your local radio station every day in exchange for two mentions a day on the air. There is a limousine company in our area that takes the morning DJ to work when he needs a lift in exchange for the DJ talking about the company on air. If you create your own ads, don't forget to ask for a 15 percent agency commission, because they'd be paying it to an agency anyhow. Make sure you get the discount.

Nuts and Bolts of Radio Advertising

1. If you don't have the attention of the listener within five seconds, you've failed.

2. Consider all the radio tools available, a voice alone or several voices, background music or foreground jingle, and sound effects in great abundance.

3. Mention your name at least five times within a 30-second spot. People won't remember it as well otherwise.

4. Develop a radio persona so people know it's you regardless of the thrust of your radio message or the sound of the spot. Get yourself an identity. Someone should be able to identify your ad even if they miss the beginning or the end of the spot.

5. Commit to only one or two stations. You need to repeat yourself to the same people, and you can only do that by focusing on a few stations at a time.

☞ **Your Midair Advertising:** If you want to get noticed, hire a blimp, maybe not the Goodyear blimp, but there are many smaller blimps. It will probably cost you a lot but the value for your money is unbeatable. There is no better way to break through the clutter. People have a mystical attraction for things in the sky and a blimp is your very own UFO.

The Goodyear blimp is an attraction, not just an advertisement. Goodyear gets billions of dollars worth of exposure from their blimp every year. Blimps, hot air balloons, and sky writing are good ways to go if you want to build name brand recognition. You cannot tell a story with a blimp but you can sure make an impression.

If you are a company trying to break into a market or an industry, fly a blimp over the crowd of the PJ Masters Golf Tournament, instant name recognition. Of course you can always advertise on the tournament's television broadcast instead, but for the same amount of money you will reach ten times the people with a blimp and the blimp will have far more impact.

The single longest running promotion used by the 7Up Company is a hot air balloon in the shape of a 7Up can that was created by Aerostar International. They take the balloon all over the country setting it up at festivals, and sporting events. When they sponsor a fun-run or an outdoor carnival, the balloon is there. 7Up has found that people will stop and get out of their cars just to take pictures of the inflated can. How many billboard advertisers can say that? The balloon attracts crowds, creates a positive image for the 7Up Company, and positions the product as fun and light hearted.

Many companies are using variations of this approach. Wendy's has an inflatable frosty. At Jamba Juice we got a lot of bang for our buck when we made a giant 20-foot Jamba Juice smoothie cup. It was very bright and got a lot of attention. These are the cold air inflatables that are even more affordable than the flying helium balloons. These are units that sit on the ground and have fans blowing air into them. They range in size from 6 to 60 feet tall. You can purchase one that is six feet tall in the shape of a can for under $500. The average size is 30 feet and the cost is between $10,000.00 and $15,000.00. That may seem like a lot, but it is money well spent.

You could also consider flying a tethered blimp outside your store or restaurant. This type ranges in size from 12 to 40 feet and can be flown up to 150 feet above your store. Paint one with your logo or slogan and watch your store's recognition soar with it.

The owner of a fireworks store in Alabama bought a custom helium blimp from Aerostar International. The blimp was the only part of their marketing plan they changed from one year to the next. They kept the same yellow pages ad, the same outdoor billboard and the same direct mail package, all they added was a helium blimp that cost them $895.00 and they saw a 15 percent increase in business.

Look into the new high tech features of blimps and airships to increase your exposure. There are night blimps that flash messages in neon and new sky writing techniques that work just like dot matrix printers, making your message suddenly appear in the sky like magic.

There is also the new large screen television set perched on the News Day building in New York Square. No. It does not fly, but it achieves the same purpose, high impact and recognition from mid-air advertising.

☞ **Your Television Advertising:** Guerrillas know that television advertising has impact. More than any other medium, TV can generate an emotional reaction in viewers. With the average household watching seven hours of television everyday you are guaranteed an audience.

TV can serve many purposes for your company. Use it to build store traffic, establish a brand name, or position yourself with consumers. Given all the advantages you are surely aware that television advertising is rather expensive. For that reason, make sure you pick your shots carefully. A 30 second spot on the Super Bowl will cost nearly a million dollars. Faced with these forbidding numbers, Guerrillas have responded in two way: Some like Master Lock have decided to take their entire TV budget and spend it on just one ad. The value of repetition is lost but Master Lock's executives do get good seats at the Super Bowl.

Smaller guerrillas have abandoned TV because they think it is too expensive, but television may just be worth reconsidering. With the explosion of cable TV there are too many stations chasing too few advertisers. You might find 30 channels broadcasting to one neighborhood. Each station runs about ten ads in a given half hour. That is 600 ads in an hour, a huge opportunity for the Guerrilla. If you explore the opportunities on cable networks and non-affiliated stations you will find that you can buy a minute of TV advertising for as little as $100.00. Of course you will not get nationwide coverage on Seinfeld but so what.

Test your ads and soon you will find yourself at the right balance of budget and frequencies.

Nuts and Bolts of Television Advertising

A good television commercial is:

1. Entertaining. A commercial that entertains is memorable.

2. Clear. The viewer understands the message immediately.

3. Visual. The viewer can see the message.

4. High quality. The quality of the commercial reflects the quality of the product. If your commercial is poor quality and obviously cheap, people who see it will assume the product being sold is just as shoddy.

5. Truthful. A commercial full of obvious exaggerations will backfire on you.

6. A call to action. Instruct the viewer to do something with the information you have just given him. Ideally go to the store and buy your product.

7. Filled with content not just special effects. Special effects get attention but the content is what sells the product.

8. Uses actors or voiceovers that inspire confidence. Do not cast your kid as the star.

More Nuts and Bolts of Television Advertising

You need to test commercials before you run them. Do this in the following ways:

1. Watch it with the sound turned off. Can you still figure out who it is for and how to respond?

2. Show it to a room full of 12-year-olds. Do they stop talking long enough to watch it? Then ask them what it is about.

3. Watch the commercial 20 times in a row. Is it so abrasive you become angry?

4. Watch just the first half or just the second half of the commercial. Do you still understand what is being sold?

☞ **Your Movie Commercials:** Certainly you've seen these while sitting in the movie theater waiting for the previews, which themselves are ads. Movie commercials flash-up on the screen for eight to ten seconds at a time. With this advertising you definitely have a captive audience and your ad is bigger than life on a giant screen.

The challenge with this type of marketing is that unless you have a hook or offer the prospect a discount for mentioning your ad or at least have them present their movie stub, it is a tough thing to track.

Movie commercials work much like billboards in that companies offering them generally want a six-month contract. This type of contract makes it very difficult to test the effectiveness but you can generally get on eight screens for about $900.00 per month. Keep in mind this works best if your place of business is in the same neighborhood as the theaters, but it is not mandatory, just more targeted.

☞ **Your Barter Options:** A great way to save impressive sums of money and get exposure is through bartering. Your local radio station or newspaper may not want what you are selling but they do want something. In all likelihood, you can trade with someone who has what they want. If so, you will get your media ads for a fraction of their usual costs since you will be paying with your own services or goods at the full retail price.

Here is an example of bartering. A stereo dealer wanted to advertise on radio but he could not afford the cost. He offered to trade recording equipment but the station was not interested. The station was interested, however, in constructing a new lobby. The stereo dealer found a contractor who wanted new stereo equipment. The result, the contractor received $5,000.00 worth of stereo equipment, the radio station got its new lobby, and the stereo dealer received $5,000.00 worth of radio time. The good news is that the dealer's cost was only $2,500.00 in equipment.

There are companies out there that specialize in bringing businesses together who want to barter services. Trade Source, for example, is in Phoenix. I used them for several years in one of my businesses. I would give them vouchers toward any service that I provided. In exchange, I could choose from a list of businesses in the organization and get vouchers of theirs. They advertised within the group to all members. You not only save money this way but get exposure and people coming to you that you normally would not and it costs you nothing in advertising.

Section Three

GUERRILLA EXECUTION

YOUR MARKETING BUDGET

NOTE: Be sure you access the Franchise Training Center online for the worksheets that correspond with this section.

NOW THAT YOU have all this information the most important thing is for you to turn it into action and execute what you have learned. Just prior to determining the strength and scope of your marketing launch, it is critical to determine the amount of money and resources you are willing to invest.

Let's talk about your marketing budget. When it comes to marketing planning, preparing, and following a marketing plan, your budget is crucial. Too often we see business owners who market on a month-by-month basis with no rhyme or reason. If business is slowing down, they increase their marketing. If business picks up, they stop. The challenge with this is that every business has a natural rhythm, levels of sales and marketing that are self-sustaining. If you do not do enough marketing you wither and die. If you do too much marketing, you waste marketing dollars or generate more business than you can handle.

The best way to budget for marketing is to choose a percentage of your sales. A good rule of thumb is 10 percent. That may come as a shock to those of you who are not committed at all to a budgeted amount for marketing. If that is the case, you have a great future to look forward to. If you are not currently spending more than 1 percent on marketing, can you imagine what will happen when you increase that slowly to 10 percent or more? You are in for an exciting adventure. With the information you've learned you will no longer be randomly throwing ads out there when the Val Pac rep comes by. You will have a plan, a calendar, a budget, and target market.

The bigger your budget, the faster you will get results, but be careful. Raise it gradually. I learned the hard way once by putting so much marketing out there we could not handle the business effectively. Also, a positive cash flow is key. Realize that it will take a few months to get results from money spent.

While you may experience some immediate results, remember, marketing takes time. Whatever percentage of sales you are currently spending, I recommend you double it, up to 10 percent. If you are at 1 percent, you go to 2 percent. If you are currently spending 4 percent, go to 8 percent. However, if you are at 8 percent, first of all, great job, second, you are pretty committed right now, third, just move to 10 percent. Stay at each level for two to three-month periods to get adjusted to the increase in business.

So what do you do if your business is not steady or if you just started a new business? The first step is to project out how much you would like to do in sales over the next year and take a percentage of that. Take some time with this. Really put some thought into making sure you pick a number you can stick with. Once you complete this, you are ready to fill in your marketing calendar and launch your marketing attack.

By now you should have your budget established and know what you are going to invest in your marketing. Also, by now, you should have completed your seven-step-marketing plan. You have gone through the 100+ weapons and categorized them into one of the four categories. Excellent!

YOUR MARKETING CALENDAR

YOUR GUERRILLA MARKETING CALENDAR will assist you in launching your marketing vehicles. These will drive you to your marketing goals in a structured and well thought out manner.

By using a marketing calendar effectively you will not only be able to successfully coordinate all your marketing efforts, you will also be able to effectively budget for all of your marketing ventures. Your marketing calendar, if used effectively, can keep you on track, making sure that you are using every opportunity you have to market without a lapse in your efforts. Your marketing calendar will help you to avoid yo-yo marketing which we referred to earlier as marketing aggressively when sales are low and less aggressively when sales are high.

As with your seven-step-marketing plan, your marketing calendar does not need to be fancy to be effective. It is simple, targeted and effective.

The purpose of your calendar is to see where you have been and where you are going with your marketing. It will give you a way to grade your marketing and its effectiveness. Your marketing calendar is a management tool. This tool helps you get things done and measure both key management activities.

Another benefit of your marketing calendar is that it will help you plan or spot efficiencies and synergies. Perhaps combining initiatives will help you take advantage of lower costs or improve effectiveness of marketing weapons to be deployed simultaneously.

Another great advantage is that your calendar will provide you with a great visual. You will be able to see very clearly if you have spaced your marketing out properly and consistently instead of stacking on top of each other.

Remember, consistent persistent marketing works. Blasts of marketing are less effective. Effective marketing calendars break down the weeks of a year and address the marketing activities that will take place in each week. A calendar will best be used if it is specific, spelling out individual promotions or events, including the marketing cost for each event. By doing this it is easy to see at a glance which events and strategies were productive and on target. This will help you effectively plan your marketing future.

One of the biggest differences between the Guerrilla marketer and the casual marketer is how the calendar is used for marketing measurement. You should review the activity from your calendar often checking the efficiencies and inefficiencies. The more regularly you do this the more you will recognize patterns of things that really work well for your business. As you rate the effectiveness of the weapons use a simple rating of effectiveness from one to ten with ten being very effective. You will repeat the marketing that scores between five and ten and reevaluate or eliminate those that fall below five.

Using the sample calendar as a reference we will now discuss and offer suggestions on how to use your marketing calendar. At the top of each section there is a place for you to write the month. As you can see, this one has been created with two months per page. It was also created to leave enough space for you to track many different marketing weapons since we suggest you use several at a time to really create and maintain synergy.

Under the month you will find weeks. You can break this down to one week or group two weeks together. For example, for two weeks on one line you may put weeks of January 1 to January 14 if you do not market weekly. If you simply want to track it by month, you can use the *weeks of* column for what days the marketing hits the market. Again, this is flexible. Find what works for you and your company. The most important thing is for you to fill out the calendar, use it, and stick with it. Stay committed.

Next to the *weeks of* column, you have the *marketing thrust or offer*. This refers to perhaps a particular sandwich or burger you are highlighting that month if you are in the restaurant business. It may be a particular service you are highlighting if you are in the service business. It may be a seasonal flavor of fruit smoothie you are highlighting if you are in the smoothie business. If you do not highlight a product or service you can put the offer of your marketing here. For example, are you offering a free consultation, or a buy-one-get-one-free widget? Write whatever it is.

The next column is dedicated to the specific marketing weapon you will use to promote the offer. If you are writing an article for U.S. News, that would be the weapon. If you are using a direct-mail postcard to announce a new arrival, that would be your marketing weapon.

Next is *length of impact*. This refers to how long the selected medium will run or how long the offer runs. The purpose of this is to try and gauge the type of traffic you will have coming into your business. If you use a weekly newsletter the length would be one week. If it is a direct-mail campaign people will not all come to your business on one day unless of course you have a one-day event. Perhaps the mailing will hit at the beginning of the month and the offer expires 30 days later. In that case, you know your business will be spread out over the following 30 days so the length of the impact will be 30 days.

The next column is *reach*, also known as *distribution*. How many people are being targeted? This is generally pretty simple, depending on the medium you use. If you send out 3,000 postcards your reach is 3,000. If you advertise in a magazine that reaches 40,000 people that is your reach. The main use for this is to help you determine your cost per customer gain. Wouldn't it be great if you get down to a science how much it costs you to get a customer to buy from you with each weapon that you use? You will be able to get pretty darn close if you use tracking and effectiveness sheets.

Next we have the *investment* column. How much will the marketing cost you?

The last column is especially important. *Who is responsible* for this particular campaign, is it you or a designated Guerrilla? Who will ultimately be accountable for making sure this happens? For example, if you are going to have an open house and your General Manager is responsible for inviting people from the neighboring businesses, she is accountable. Let's say you want invitations to neighboring businesses personally hand delivered by her. If the promotion is a raging success then she is accountable. By the same token, if the promotion is a crash and burn she is accountable for that as well.

Nuts and Bolts of Your Marketing Calendar

Now that you understand the calendar, let's talk about where to specifically start.

1. Refer to your marketing weapon list. Choose those weapons you would like to use in months one through three and get them written onto your calendar. Of course you will be referring back to your budget and picking and choosing accordingly.

2. The next thing that you will do is refer to any company initiatives coming up over the next several quarters.

Most franchises have quarterly and some even monthly initiatives that you should use to guide you in your marketing. You may be working with a manufacturer that does the same. Get these on your calendar as far out as you can. Add to this list any other key dates such as your business anniversary, new product introductions, etcetera.

3. Now let's estimate the timing of the initiatives you are going to use. For example, a direct-mail postcard to a target audience once a month for six months or a block party once a month where you invite people from neighboring businesses in for a celebration, etcetera. Get them on the calendar. Keep in mind you can and should make some adjustments to your calendar over time, so do not be shy, just use pencil so you can easily adjust later. Just get started by writing these things down.

4. Now, fill in the gaps between what you have on the calendar and what your budget will allow and fill in the empty spots throughout the year.

5. The important part is this: Write on your marketing calendar review dates to grade your marketing. Revise your calendar or revisit certain initiatives. You may choose to do this monthly or every other month.

You now have your Guerrilla Marketing Calendar.

Success Concept 22

YOUR TRACKING AND EFFECTIVENESS

TRACKING OR NOT TRACKING the effectiveness of your marketing campaigns can mean the difference between successful marketing and unsuccessful marketing. This will help you understand how much it costs you to bring in a customer, which marketing methods and weapons are the most effective and cost less per customer that you brought in. It will also help you understand what marketing initiatives and weapons to use more or less of. Also, which offers work the best. And finally, which mailing lists or letters work the best of all your marketing weapons.

This is powerful. This is knowledge. This will help you spend your money so much more effectively. Access the Franchise Training Center to get a copy of your *tracking and effectiveness worksheet.* Here is how this one goes. Before you can track the effectiveness of your marketing, you need a system to track the customers as they come in. Now understand that some of the marketing you do will be long-term branding and will be almost impossible to track. However, any time you use response marketing and your customers know they are responding to an ad, you can track it. But it all starts on the front lines. So we have included a *promotion tracking sheet* in the Franchise Training Center as well for you to use as a model as you see fit. Because to be able to fill out the tracking and effectiveness sheet, you need to know how many customers are responding to the ads first.

Now, the promotion tracking sheet is fairly self-explanatory and includes some basic instructions so I am not going to go into detail on that one at this time. But just know, you need to use it religiously to get accurate results. I would recommend that you make sure that the majority of customers have come in before you do a final tally on your numbers. So, for example, if a promotion runs for 30 days, obviously you will wait until after day 30 to do your final analysis. But you will be tracking your responses daily on your daily tracking sheets. On the left hand side of the page, the first column is the marketing weapon you are evaluating.

The next column is the target you set out to hit with that weapon. This is important. For example, if you send out a direct mail piece to men in the city that subscribe to hunting magazine and it did not do so well, it does not mean that direct mail does not work. Perhaps you had the wrong list. So be specific here.

The next column is the offer. If you offer 50 cents off of a $10.00 product and it bombs, the weapon could have been right, the list could have been right, but the offer, wrong. So what is the offer? The next column is for the amount sent out. This is simple for direct mail but a little trickier if you do not know how much you send out. For a magazine, again it would be the number of distribution.

The next column is the most simple. How much did it cost you for that initiative? Now here is the fun column, your cost per customer. You determine this by dividing the amount of money you spent on the initiative by the amount of customers that responded. Now, you and only you, can determine how much a customer is worth. If it costs you $3.00 per customer, is that good? But if it costs you $50.00 per customer, is that good? You need to figure out how much a customer is worth to you. Now you have the cost per customer. It is time to give that marketing initiative a grade. A, B, C, D or F. You need to determine what you consider good. Generally, I keep the A's and B's and really focus on them until they all become A's. If they die down over time, I will address the C's but never touch the D's or F's. They go away forever.

So that leads us to the next question. When to halt the market attack? Well, the day you close the doors of your business is the only smart time to halt a guerrilla marketing attack, no other day is a good day for quitting. A concept for you to embrace is that a guerrilla marketing attack is never ending. It has a beginning, a middle but never an end for it is a process. You improve it, perfect it, change it, even pause it but you never stop it completely.

Of all the steps to succeeding with the guerrilla market attack this one takes the most time. You spend a relatively brief time developing the attack and inaugurating it but you spend the life of your business maintaining, monitoring and improving your marketing attack. At no point should you ever take anything for granted. Don't fall into the pit of self-satisfaction because your attack is working. Never forget that other motivated competitors are studying you and doing their utmost to surpass you in the marketing arena.

Success Concept 23

THE WORTH OF A CUSTOMER

THERE ARE SEVERAL VARIABLES with this one. How long do you think a customer will patronize your business? That is the golden question and it depends on several variables, like your customer service, the quality of your product or service, etc. We can come to an educated guess for the purpose of figuring out how much it is worth paying to get a new customer. I will teach you the concept by sharing what we did in Jamba Juice.

Through surveying our customers at our locations we observed a few things. The main piece of information we were going for, however, was how often the customer would come in and drink a smoothie. While it ranged from daily to once every six months, the average, which is what you want to figure out, for our customers to patronize our business was twice a week. We know that on average they spend $4.50 with each visit.

With this information we know that in a 12 month period an average customer would spend $468.00 with us. Wow. That is pretty amazing. Two times a week is 104 times per year, multiplied by $4.50. That is $468.00. So, how much am I willing to pay to get a new customer? I know that if our service is up to par and we continue to market, we can keep our customers coming in twice a week on average. Would I be willing to spend $5.00 on marketing to get a new customer? Absolutely. $10.00 per customer? That is where it is up to you, but that is the formula. How many visits per year multiplied by how much the average transaction equals the amount that customer means to you in the year. See, your high school math did come in handy.

I added another column to help you break it down to profit. Determine what percent of money you dropped to the bottom line and multiply the annual figure times the percentage. In this case, let us say I dropped 20 percent of my bottom line; $468.00 times 20 percent is roughly $94.00 in profit.

How you use this information is important and can increase effectiveness. Pass it throughout the company and use it to improve customer service. If you lose a customer due to bad service, you not only lose $468.00 a year, but what if that person tells ten people about your bad service. Because of that, those ten people never try you or your product out. That is almost $5,000.00 in potentially lost business in one year due to one bad experience. Do you get it? This information is powerful if you first track it and use it regularly.

YOUR FOLLOW-UP AND REFERRAL PLAN

GUERRILLA MARKETING PREACHES the importance of customer follow up and prospect follow-up. Why is it that most businesses lose customers? Most businesses lose customers by ignoring them. A numbing 68 percent of all business lost in America is lost due to apathy and lack of follow-up after the sale.

Misguided business owners think that marketing is over once they made the sale. Wrong, wrong, wrong! Marketing begins once you have made the sale. It is of monumental importance to you and your company that you understand this concept. First of all, understand how guerrillas view follow-up. They make it a part of their DNA because they know it now costs six times more to sell something to a new customer than to an existing customer.

We have talked a lot about how the best and the most inexpensive way to get new business is to get referrals. Word of mouth is the best, but it takes a long time. Just plan on that business as gravy. It will come with time and excellent service on your part. But you need a plan.

You need a system in place that has you asking for referrals from your current satisfied customers. We have provided a worksheet for you to use to brainstorm how it is that you will do this. (This worksheet is found on the Franchise Training Center Website.) Keep in mind that the easiest way is simply to ask if the customer is satisfied with your service and ask who else they know that would likely benefit from your service.

There are entire courses on this subject alone, which is out of the scope of this book, but let's get started with some basics.

Nuts and Bolts of Asking for Referrals

1. What incentive can you give for people sending you referrals? Is it bribing? Absolutely. Is it wrong? Absolutely not.

2. What about offering your customers a free gift card each time they refer someone to you?

3. What about a free lunch or a free dinner?

4. Who do you know right now out of your customer base that you know is very satisfied with your product or service? Take a moment and list them on a sheet.

5. Write down a few different ways you can go about asking for referrals from them.

How Long Before Marketing Actually Works?

As we near the end of this book and you're going to start on this journey, it's important that you understand this. How long does it take for a prospect to become a customer? Well, let's first look into the chemistry of prospects. Prospects are like you except that they are probably doing business with one of your competitors. Ouch.

Fortunately for you, that competitor likely doesn't know the full meaning of follow-up, based on the fact that most customers feel ignored after the sale. These are among your hottest prospects. They already do business with a company such as yours and may be disenchanted because they've been left alone after making a purchase.

That's why guerrillas identify their best prospects and then they begin the courtship process.

Most business owners contact prospects once or twice and if they don't show an interest the business owners move onto greener territories. Guerrillas continue romancing those they are courting. Eventually those prospects feel so cared for, so important, so attended to, that they switch over and begin to patronize that guerrilla who never stops courting. How long does it take until this happens? Try seven years on for size. That's the outside. It could happen in a month, even a week or less if the prospects are in the market right now and neglected by their former supplier. But it probably won't happen soon, and it most assuredly won't happen if you ignore them after contacting them once or twice.

Prospects have minds that are more open than you think. There are allegiances lost every day and allegiances gained every day. The guerrilla marketers don't lose them because they recognize the slow-motion process of gaining them. When they speak to prospects whether in person or through one of the venues of marketing, they do not talk about their business or their industries; they talk about the prospects themselves which is the topic most on the mind of prospects and one that ceaselessly interests them.

When guerrillas can talk about the problems facing their prospects they gain even more attention. And when they talk about solutions to these problems they still see things from the prospect's point of view and talk from that mindset. Give them time. Give them information. Give them attention. While you're waiting, walk a mile in their shoes so you can be better prepared to talk to them about how their feet feel.

People patronize the businesses they do for a wide variety of reasons.

- LOCATION: It is convenient.

- HABIT: We are creatures of habit.

- CONFIDENCE: People trust you.

- QUALITY: You provide the best.

- SERVICE: You stand out and make the customer feel appreciated.

- SELECTION: You offer the best of varieties.

- PRICE: You are competitive and fair.

Guerrillas build their businesses on loyal customers. Possessed with that insight, they do all in their power to maintain loyalty. That may happen with frequent buyer programs, or special events centered around customers, or with fervent follow-up through their newsletter, or maybe even with little freebies for their customers.

Many marketers create their marketing under the assumption that prospects are asking who you are. What is your product or service? When are you open? Where are you located? The real question in the prospect's mind is, "Why should I care? What's in it for me?" That's what they are really thinking. Not, "Tell me a story about you." It's, "Tell me a story about me. Tell me how you can save me time, increase my income, reduce my stress, bring more love into my life, cause people to think highly of me," etc.

Another insight possessed by guerrillas is that people patronize businesses that can offer things to change their lives for the good. Sometimes these things are huge things such as cars and computers, but usually they are not. Usually it is the service, kindness and time you give them.

Keep in mind that people are attracted to businesses that have established credibility. You get credibility with superb marketing and commitment to a plan. Marketing continues to be a blend of art, science, business, and patience. It works but it rarely works instantly. That's why the most crucial ingredient in the blend called marketing is your own patience.

CONCLUSION

AT THE BEGINNING of the book we set forth two objectives:

1. To teach you how to retain the customers you currently attract by plugging profit drains.

2. To teach you how to attract more customers, in the most effective ways, using Guerrilla Marketing tactics.

By following the "how" of both of those objectives, you will accomplish the following:

Marketing + Retention = Profits

In closing, I am reminded of this very simple, yet very profound truth: While there are thousands of proven theories and methods and formulas for success, (for marketing, for customer service, for general business, for franchise owners, etc.) they all boil down to the fundamental principle of ACTION!

To be successful as a franchise owner, you must ACT! You must EXECUTE the success concepts we've outlined.

Throughout these pages we tried to simplify your action steps by providing workspace in the book. We also provided worksheets available from the Franchise Training Center online. If you took the steps as you proceeded, I congratulate you! If you did not, I strongly encourage you to go back and begin immediately. After all, at the end of the day, you, the franchisee, are in ultimate control of your success. It's up to you. You decide by the actions you take! Get ready to thrive!

One (1) FREE Month Membership To The Franchise Training Center

www.GMarketingStrategies.com/bookpromo.html
Your Promotion Code is BOOK0812

- **24/7 access** to valuable resources online.

- **Interviews** with franchise industry experts on our radio program "Franchise Boot Camp Radio." Learn what the "best of the best" are doing to be successful.

- **1000's of Articles & Tips** on sales and marketing, leadership, increasing productivity and much more.

- **Audio & Video Clips** can be played on demand or emailed directly to you through our "Audio Pilot" program.

- **Franchise Resource Center** has downloadable worksheets and forms to save you time and money.

- **Franchise Marketing Rolodex** of preferred vendors and services

Be sure to visit our website **www.GMarketingStrategies.com**
or call 877-568-1212 to get information on:

KEYNOTE MARKETING SPEECHES & WORKSHOPS,
7 CD AUDIO PROGRAM, AND OTHER PRODUCTS